Airman Knowledge Testing Supplement for Aviation Maintenance Technician – General, Airframe, and Powerplant; and Parachute Rigger

2018

U.S. Department of Transportation
FEDERAL AVIATION ADMINISTRATION
Flight Standards Service

Preface

This testing supplement supersedes FAA-CT-8080-4F, Airman Knowledge Testing Supplement for Aviation Mechanic General, Powerplant, and Airframe; and Parachute Rigger, dated 2013. This Airman Knowledge Testing Supplement is designed by the Federal Aviation Administration (FAA) Flight Standards Service. It is intended for use by Airman Knowledge Testing (AKT) Organization Designation Authorization (ODA) Holders and other entities approved and/or authorized to administer airman knowledge tests on behalf of the FAA in the following knowledge areas:

Aviation Mechanic General—AMG
Aviation Mechanic Powerplant—AMP
Aviation Mechanic Airframe—AMA
Parachute Rigger—RIG, RMC, RMP

Contents

Appendix 1 - Aviation Mechanic General

Appendix 2 - Aviation Mechanic Powerplant

Appendix 3 - Aviation Mechanic Airframe

Appendix 4 - Parachute Rigger

APPENDIX 1

Aviation Mechanic General

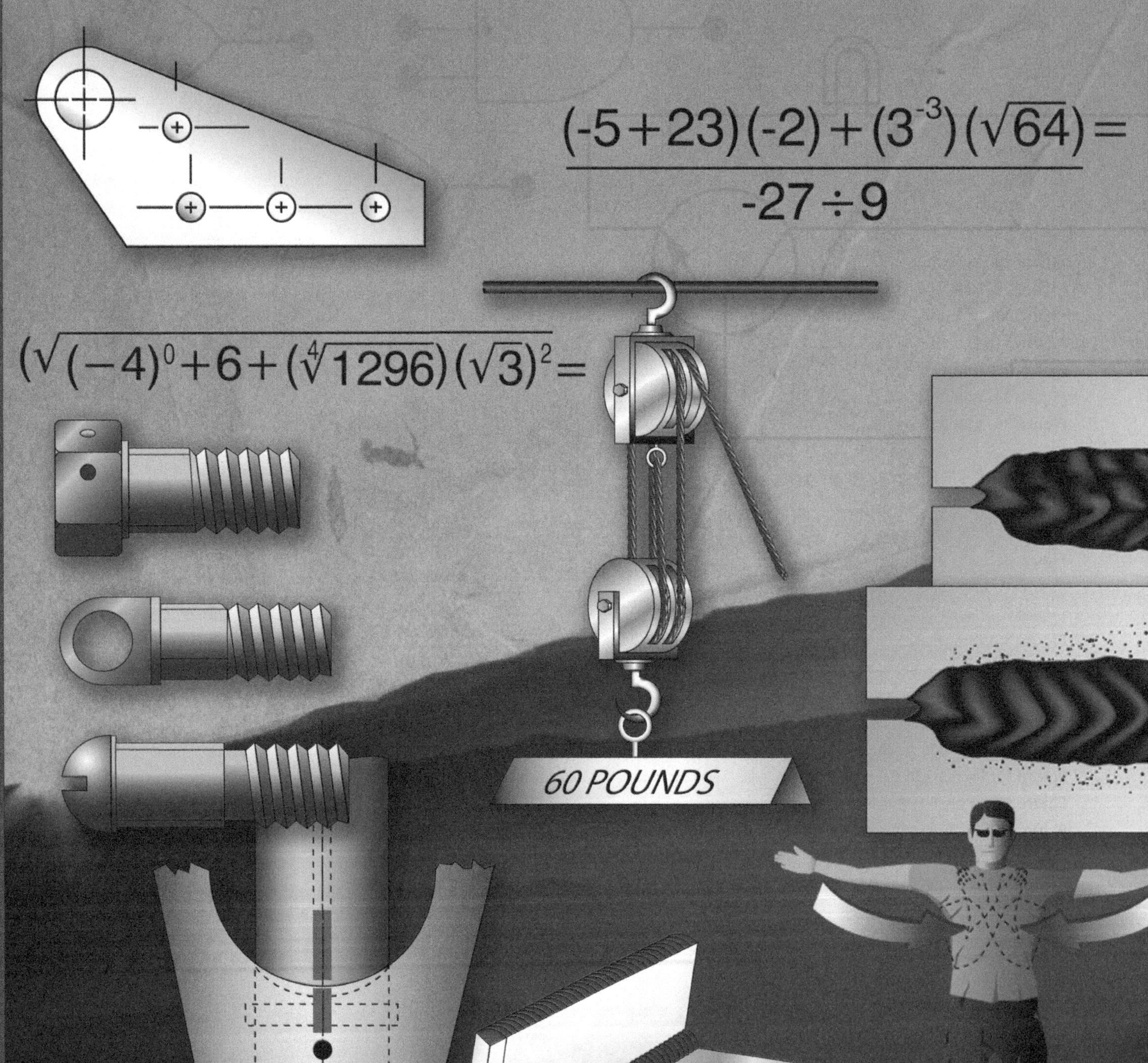

$$C_T = \frac{1}{1/C_1 + 1/C_2 + 1/C_3 \ldots}$$

Figure 1. Equation.

Appendix 1

$$C_T = \frac{1}{1/C_1 + 1/C_2 + 1/C_3}$$

Figure 2. Equation.

$$L_T = \frac{1}{1/L_1 + 1/L_2 + 1/L_3 \ldots}$$

Figure 3. Equation.

Appendix 1

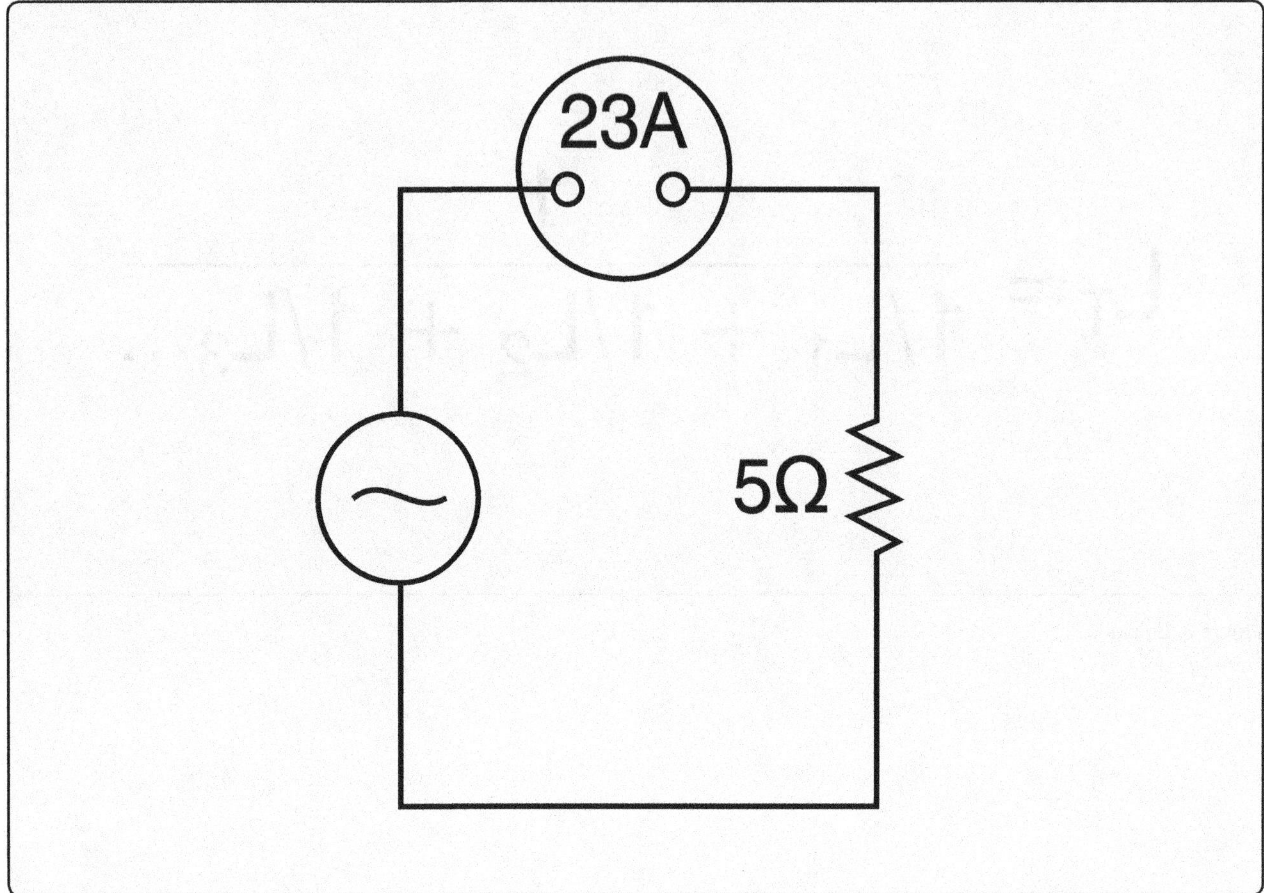

Figure 4. Circuit diagram.

$$Z = \sqrt{R^2 + (X_L - X_C)^2}$$

Z = Impedance
R = Resistance
X_L = Inductive reactance
X_C = Capacitive reactance

Figure 5. Formula.

Appendix 1

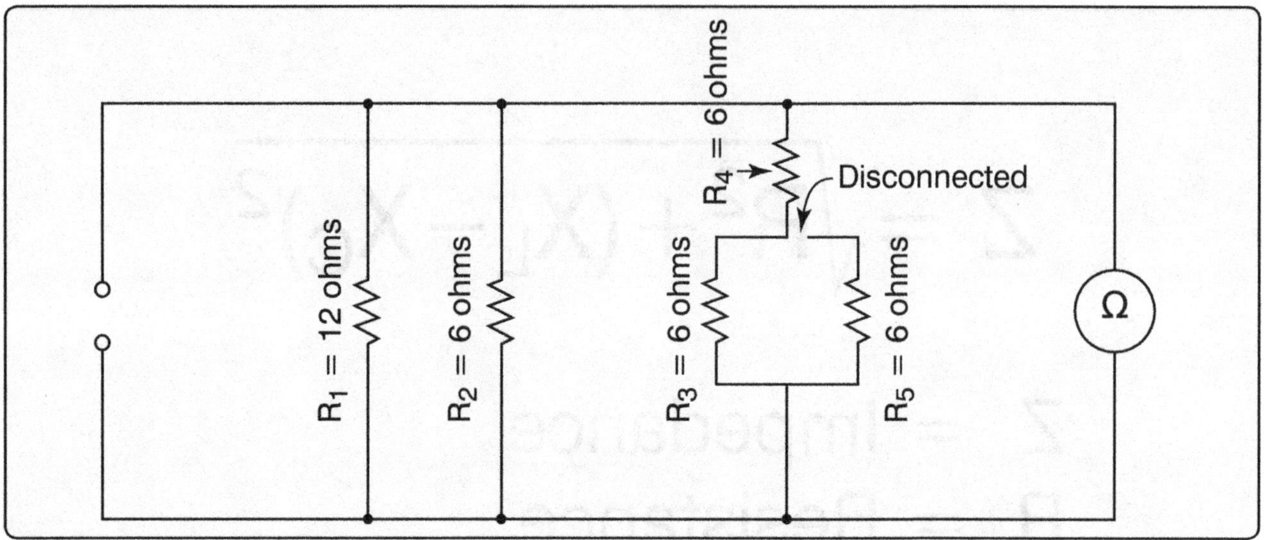

Figure 6. Circuit diagram.

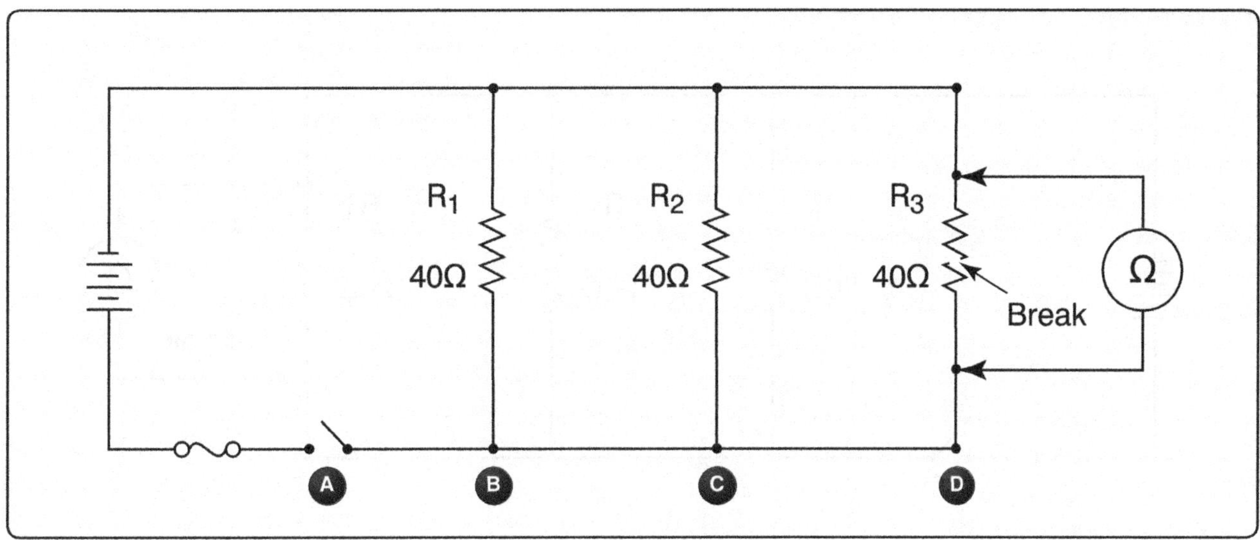

Figure 7. Circuit diagram.

Appendix 1

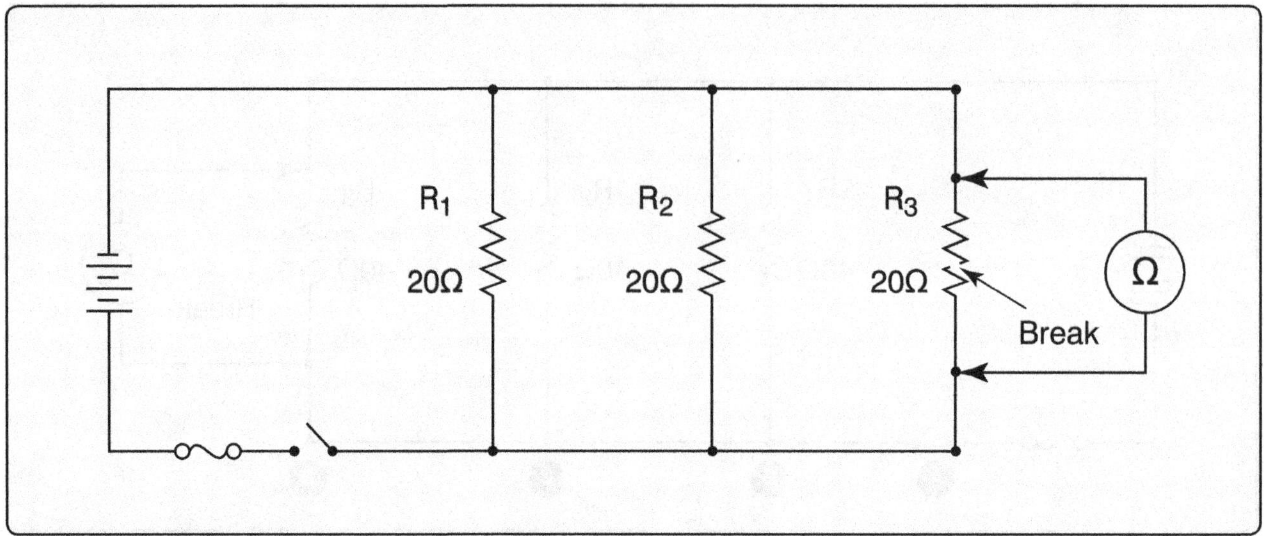

Figure 8. Circuit diagram.

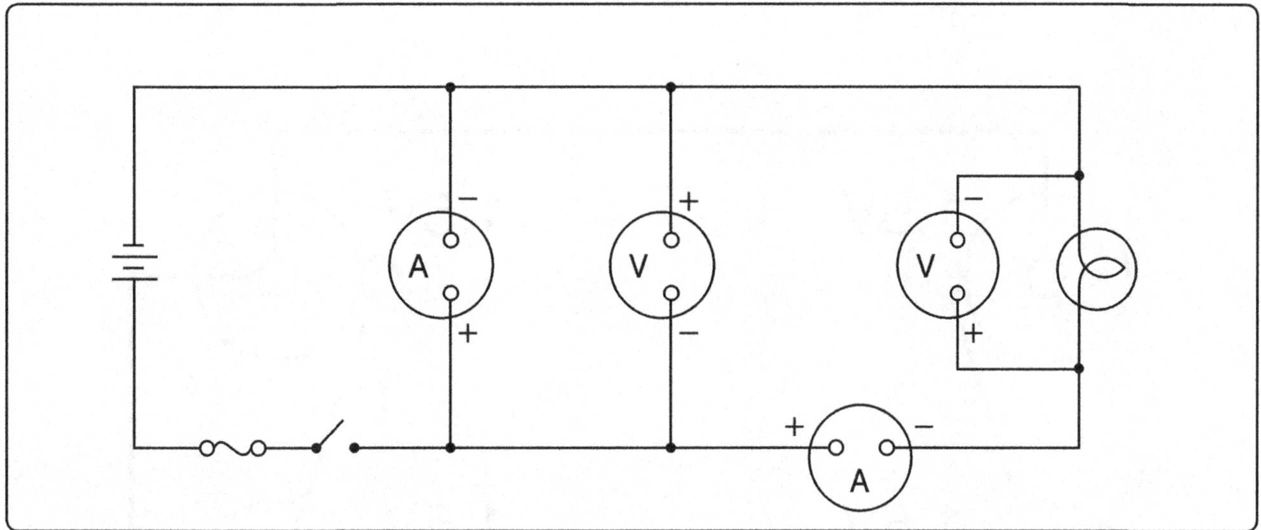

Figure 9. Circuit diagram.

Appendix 1

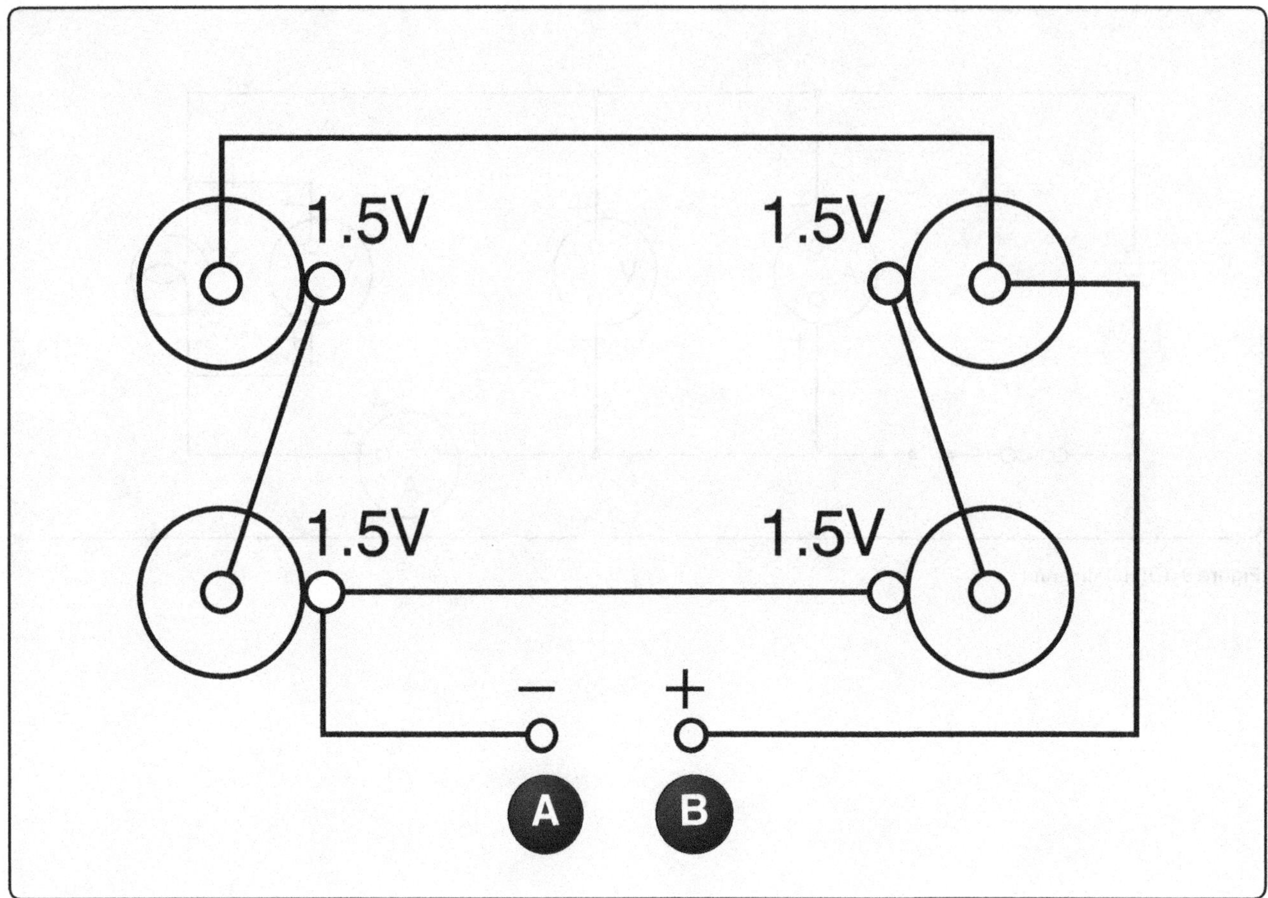

Figure 10. Battery circuit.

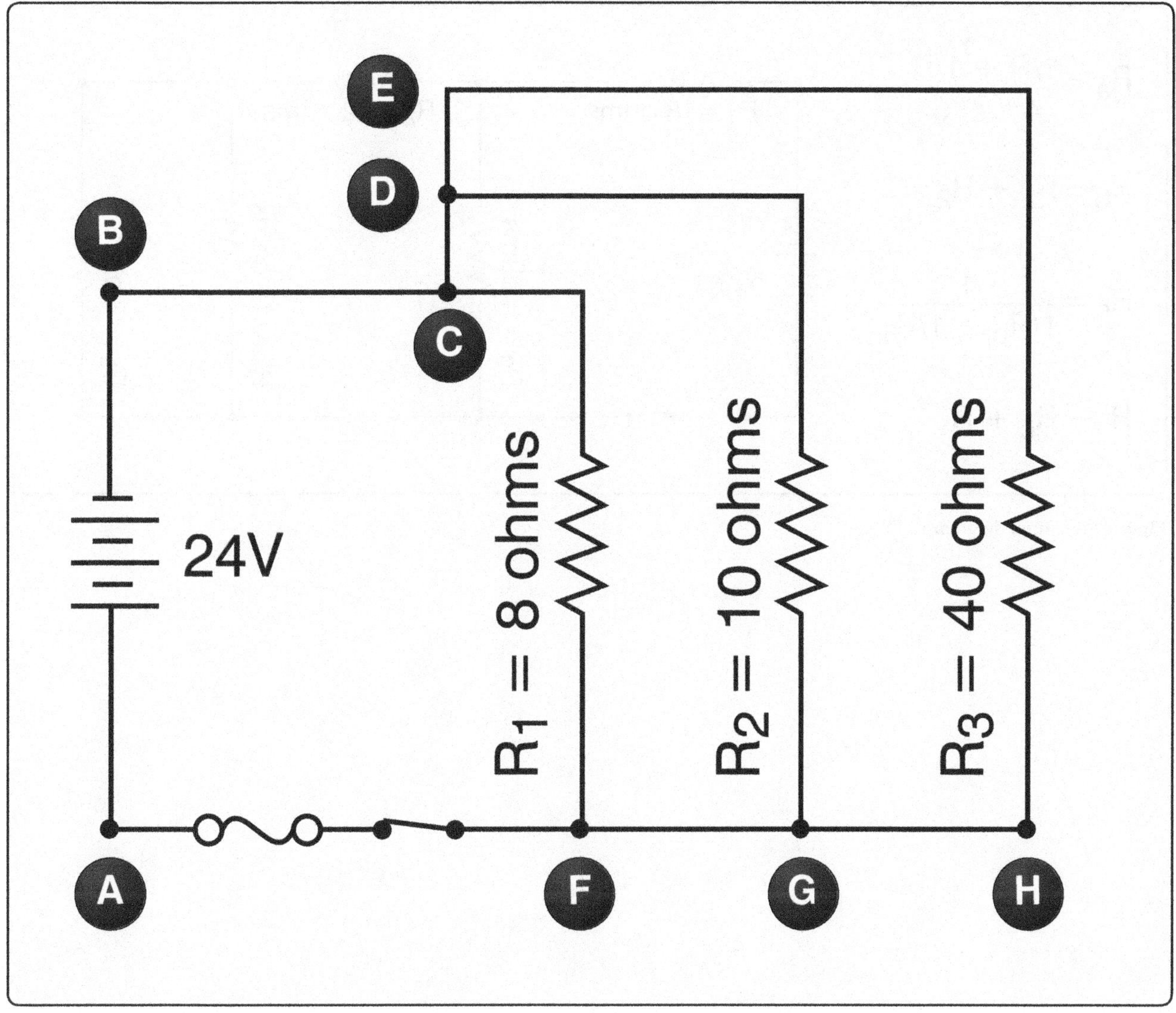

Figure 11. Circuit diagram.

Appendix 1

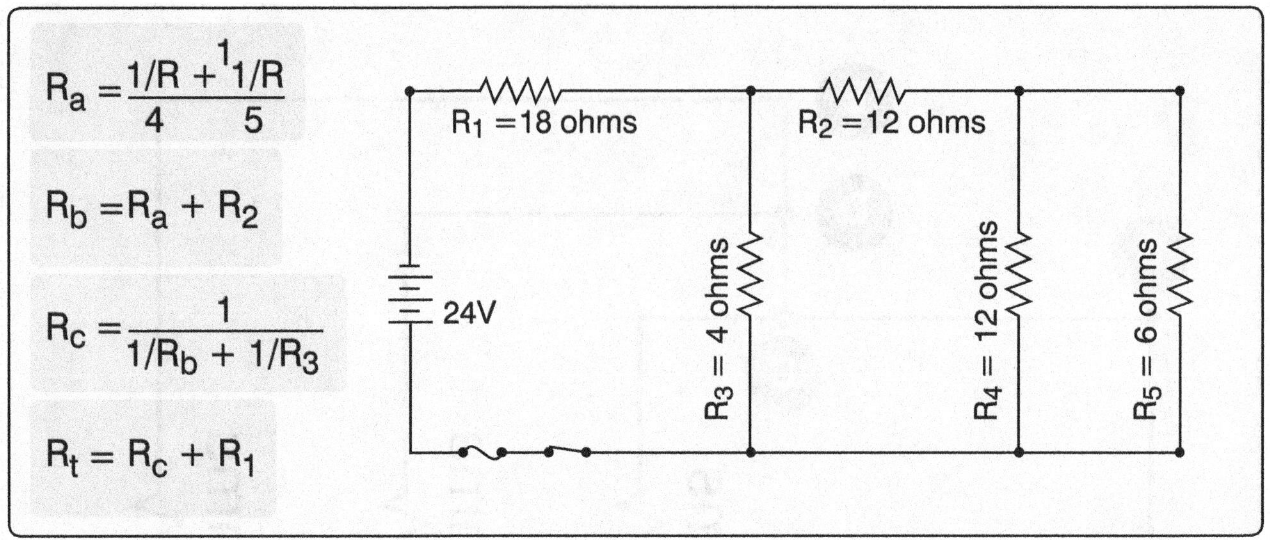

Figure 12. Circuit diagram.

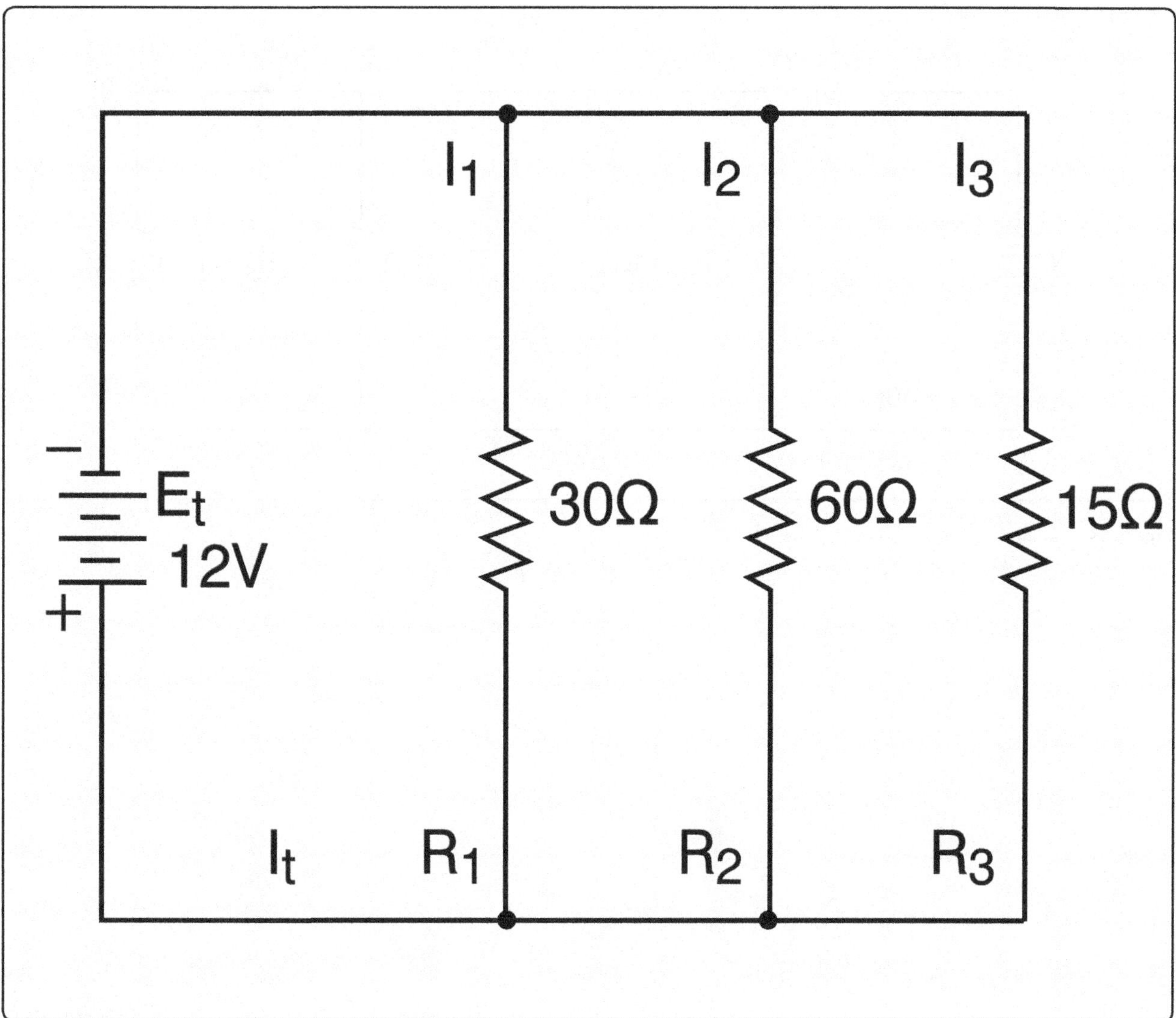

Figure 13. Circuit diagram.

Appendix 1

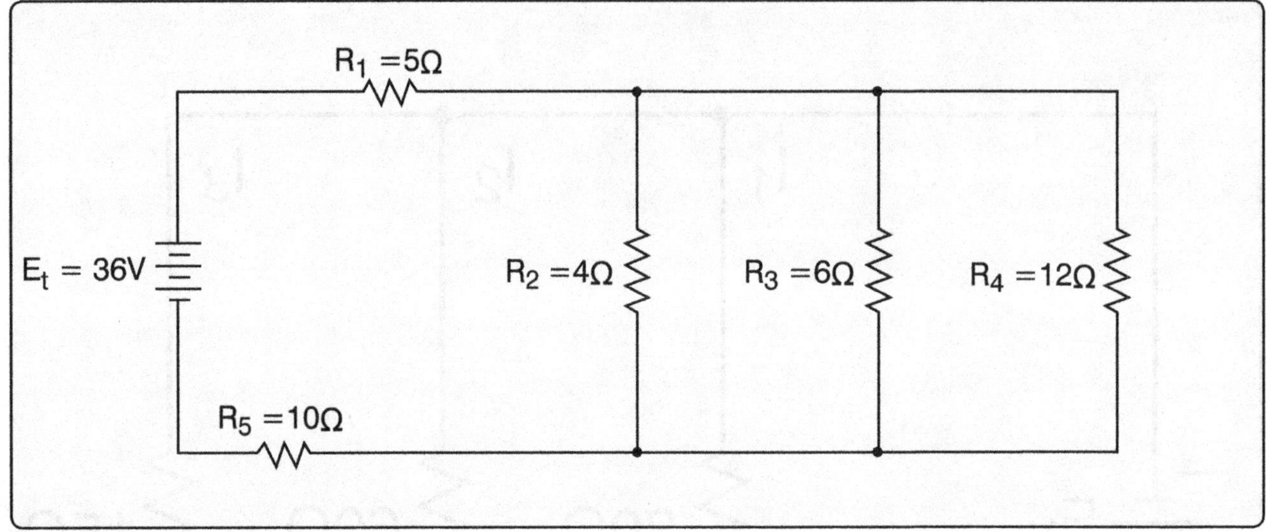

Figure 14. Circuit diagram.

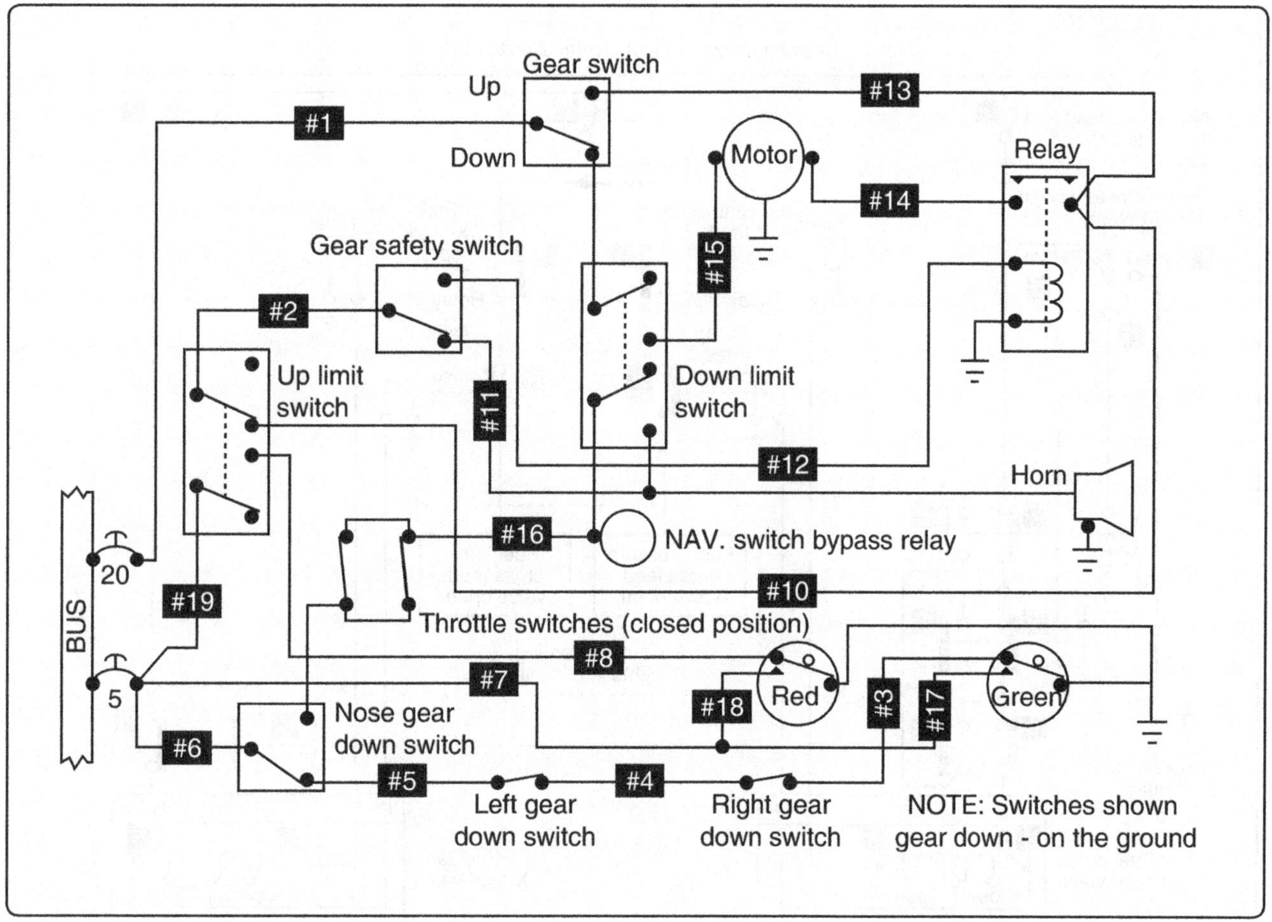

Figure 15. Landing gear circuit.

Appendix 1

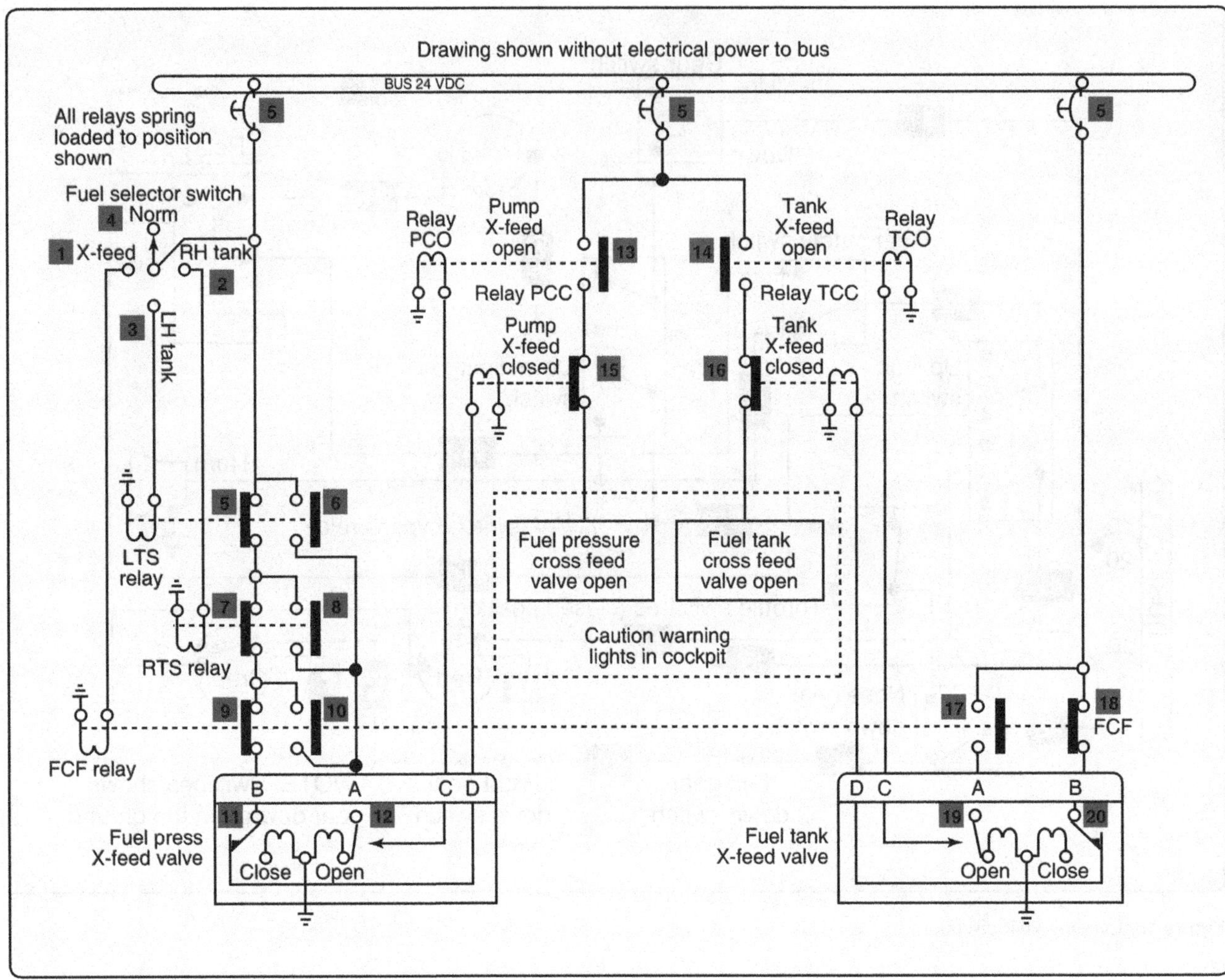

Figure 16. Fuel system circuit.

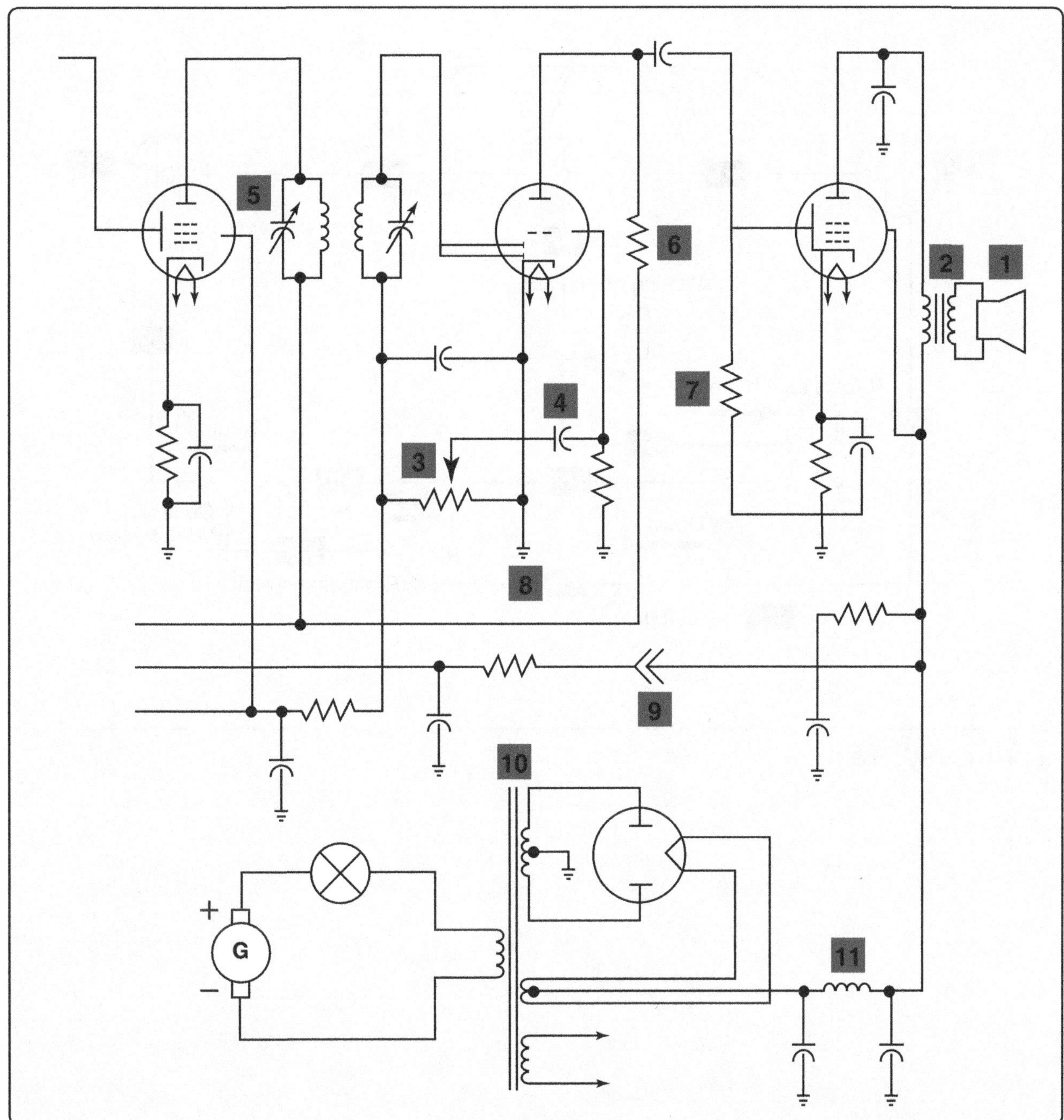

Figure 17. Electrical symbols.

Appendix 1

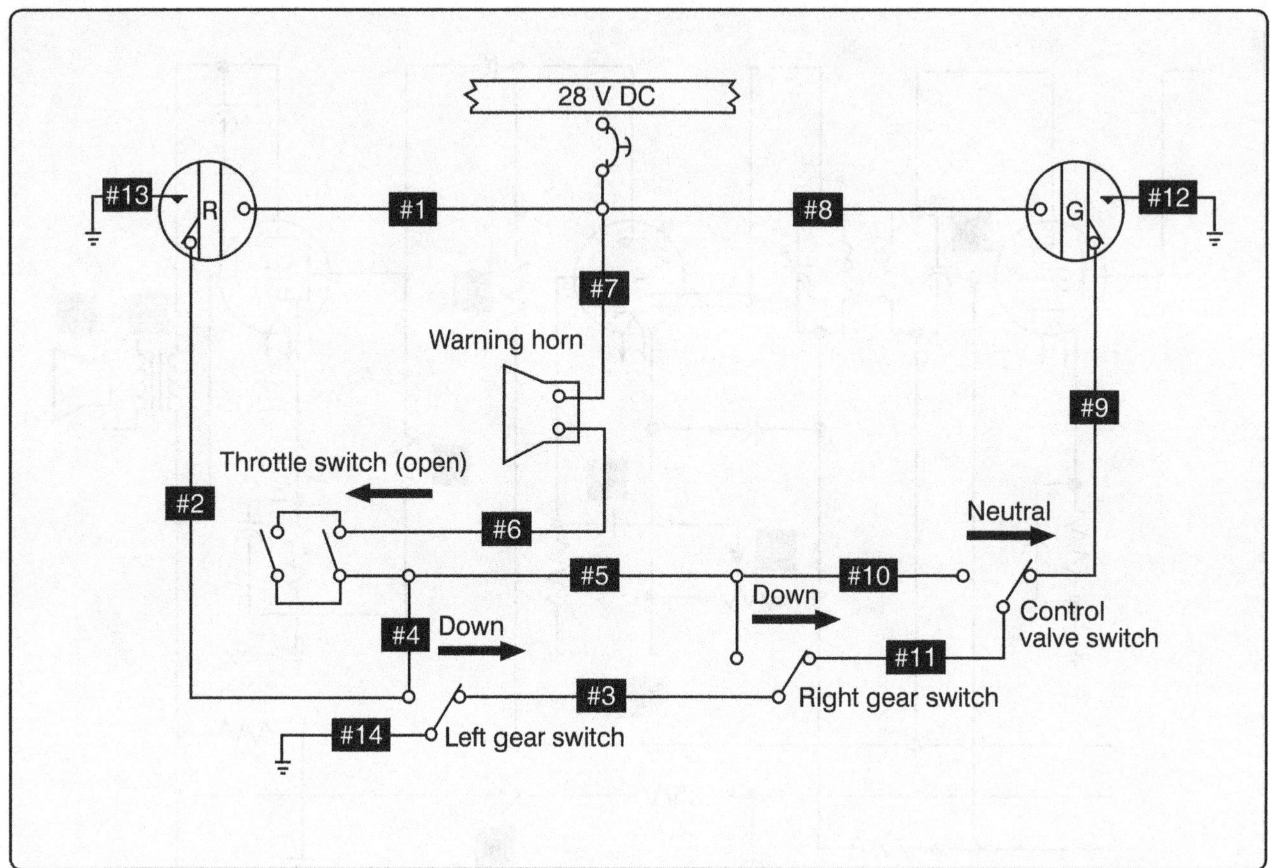

Figure 18. Landing gear circuit.

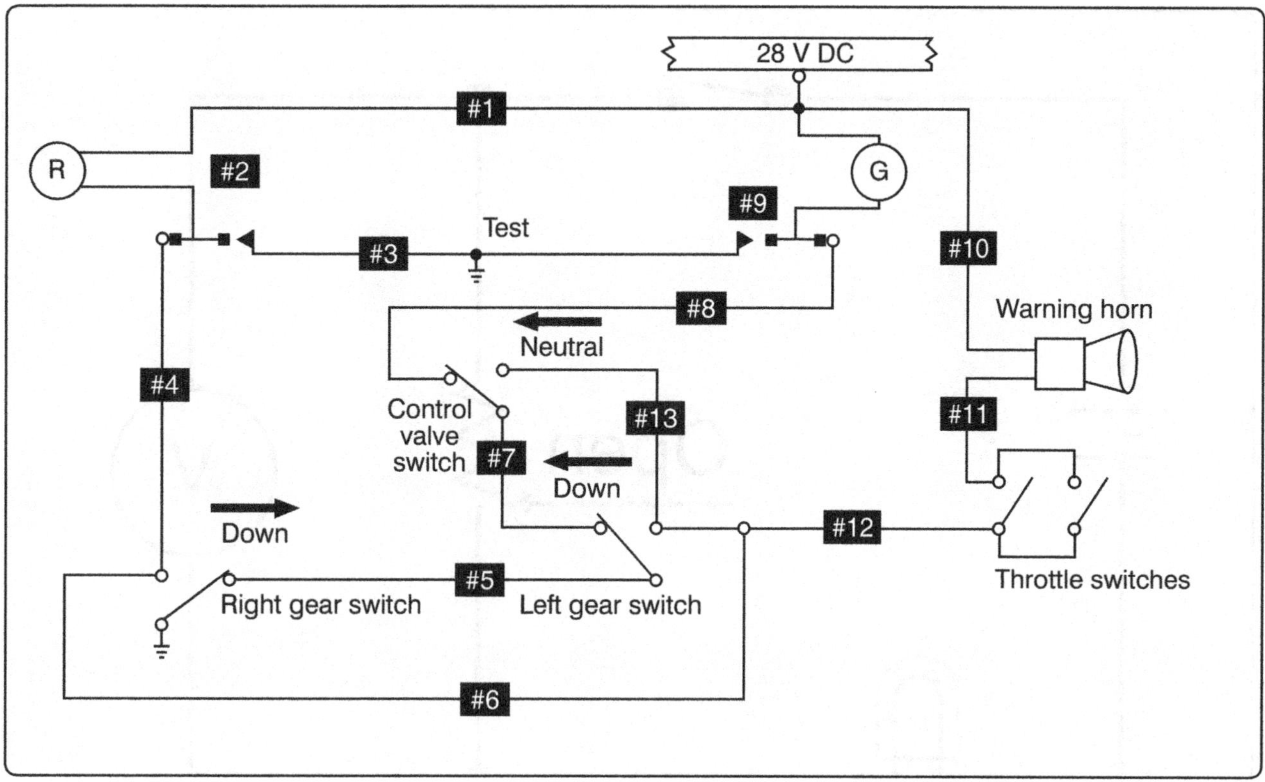

Figure 19. Landing gear circuit.

Appendix 1

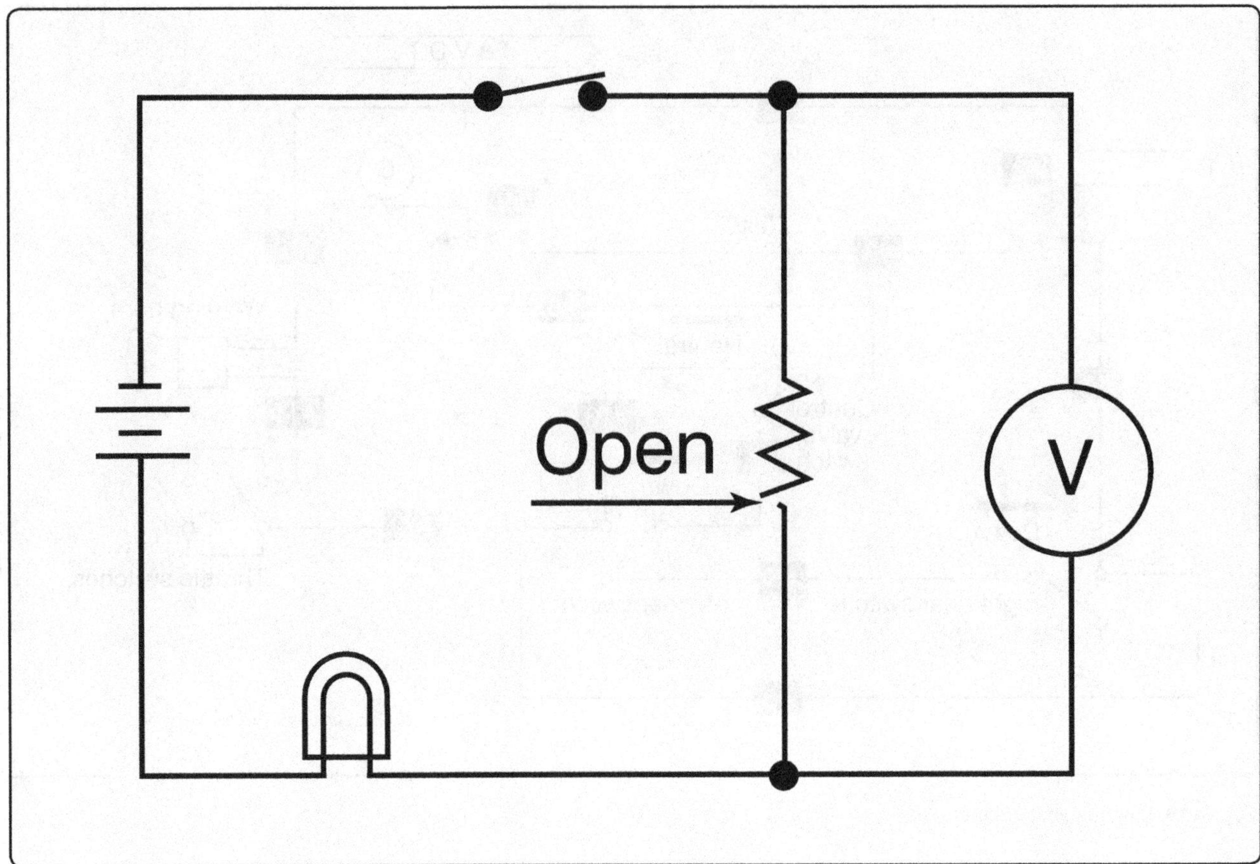

Figure 20. Circuit diagram.

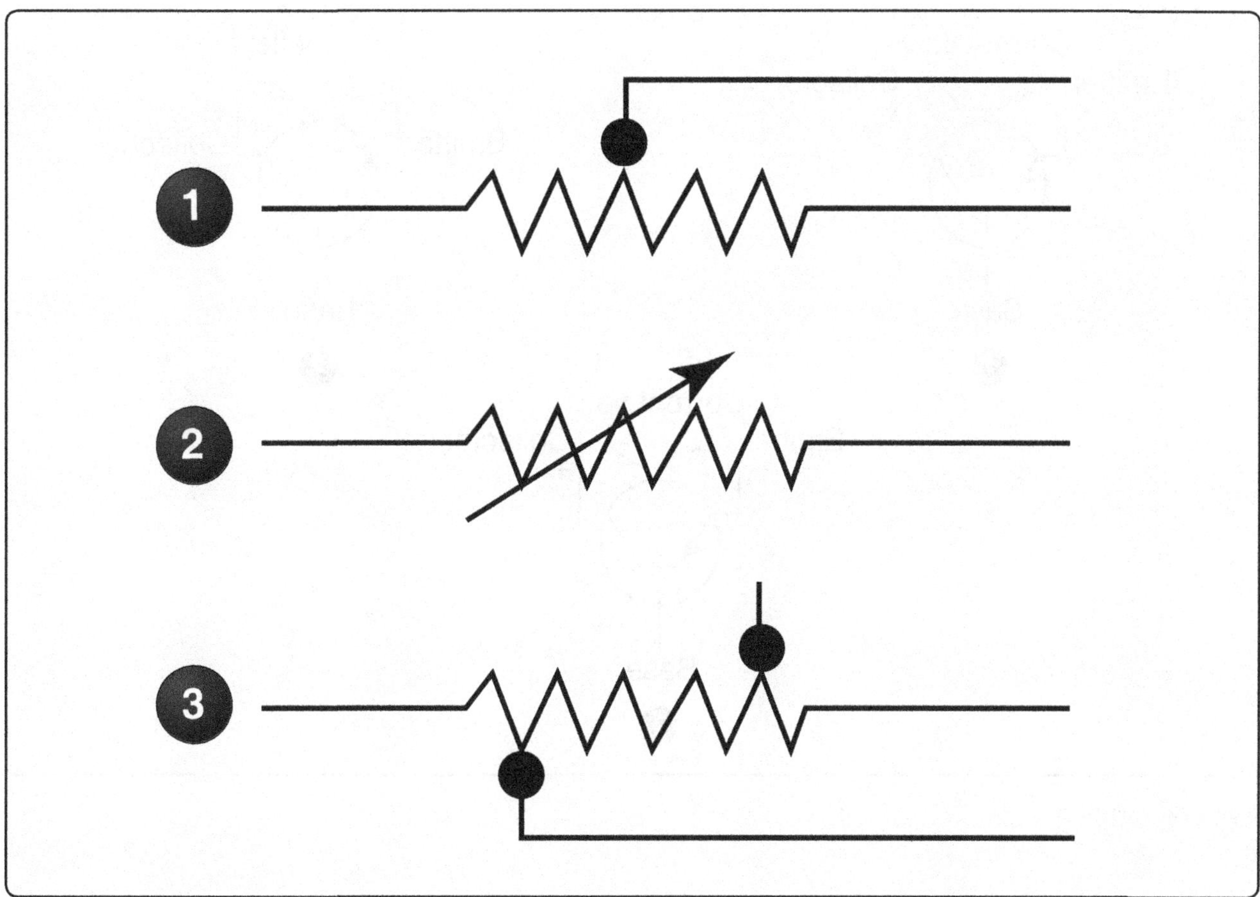

Figure 21. Electrical symbols.

Appendix 1

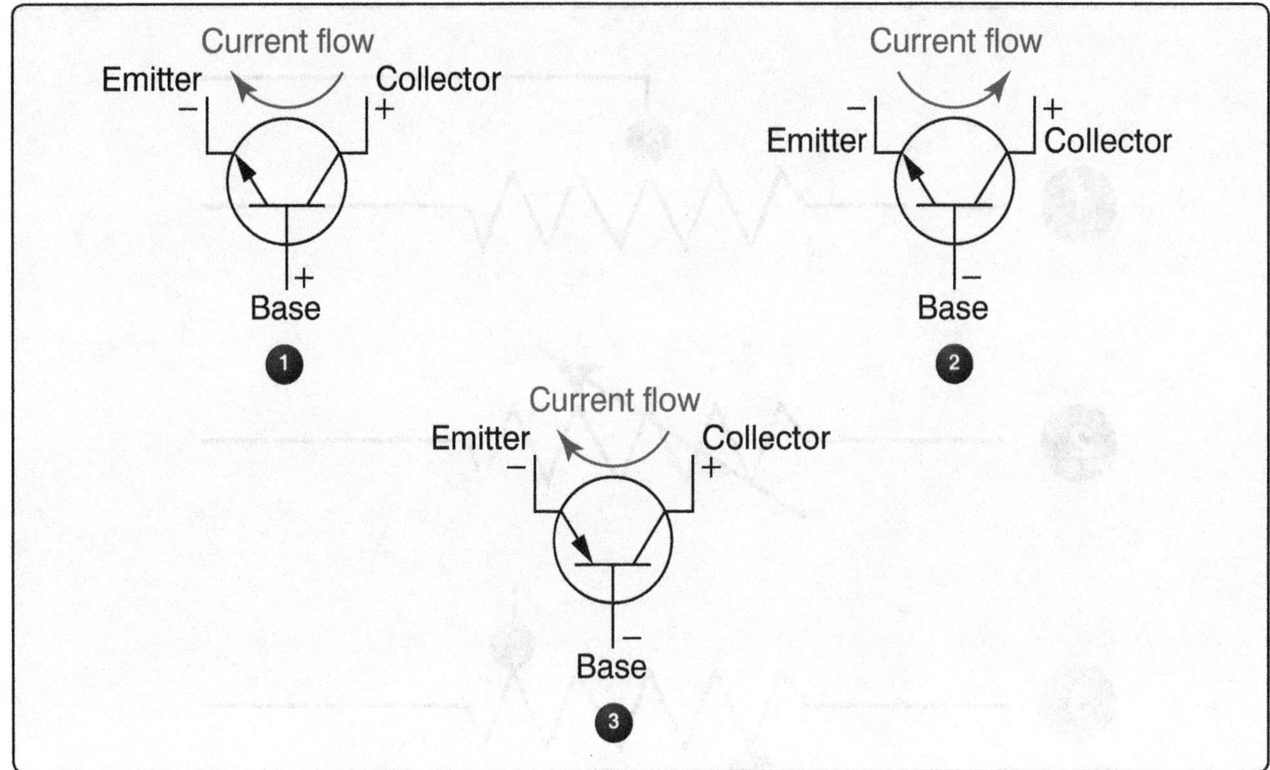

Figure 22. Transistors.

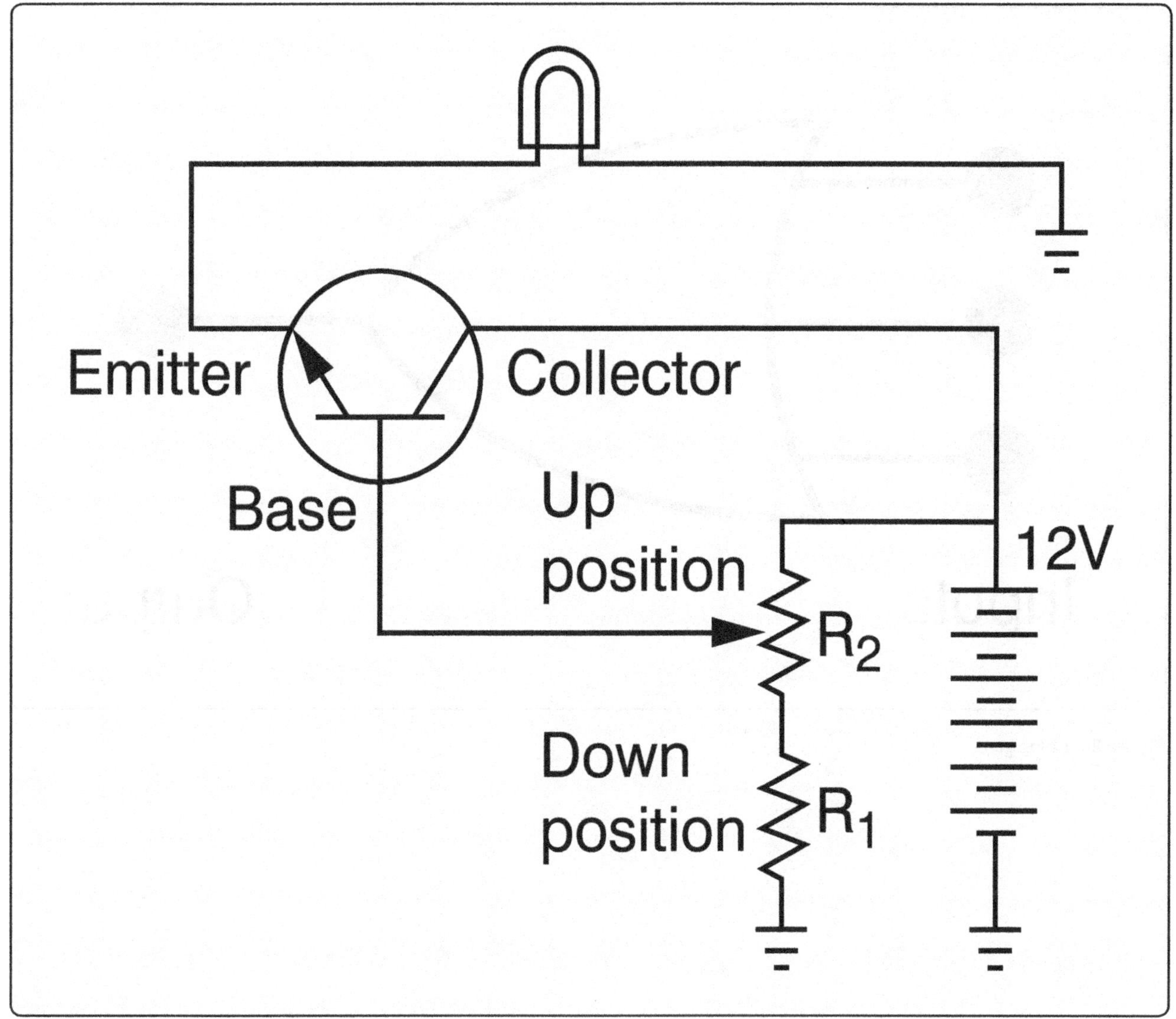

Figure 23. Transistorized circuit.

Appendix 1

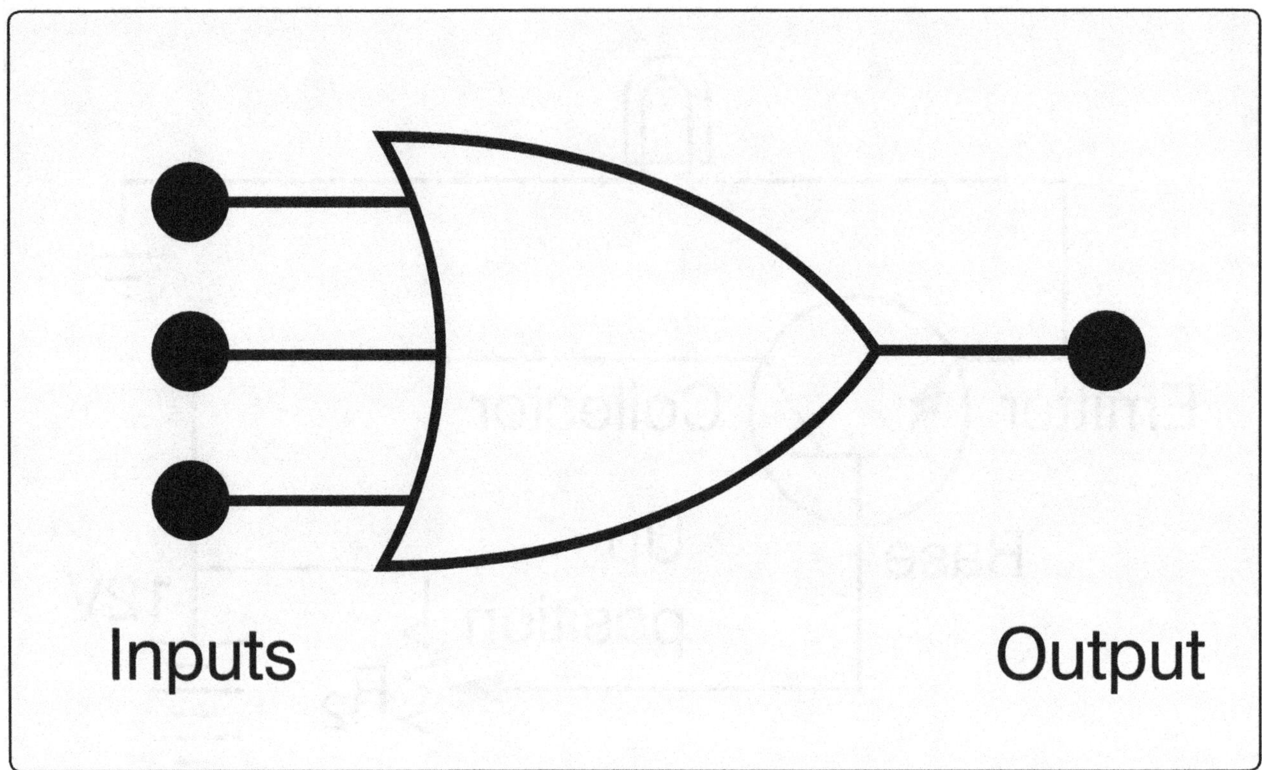

Figure 24. Logic gate.

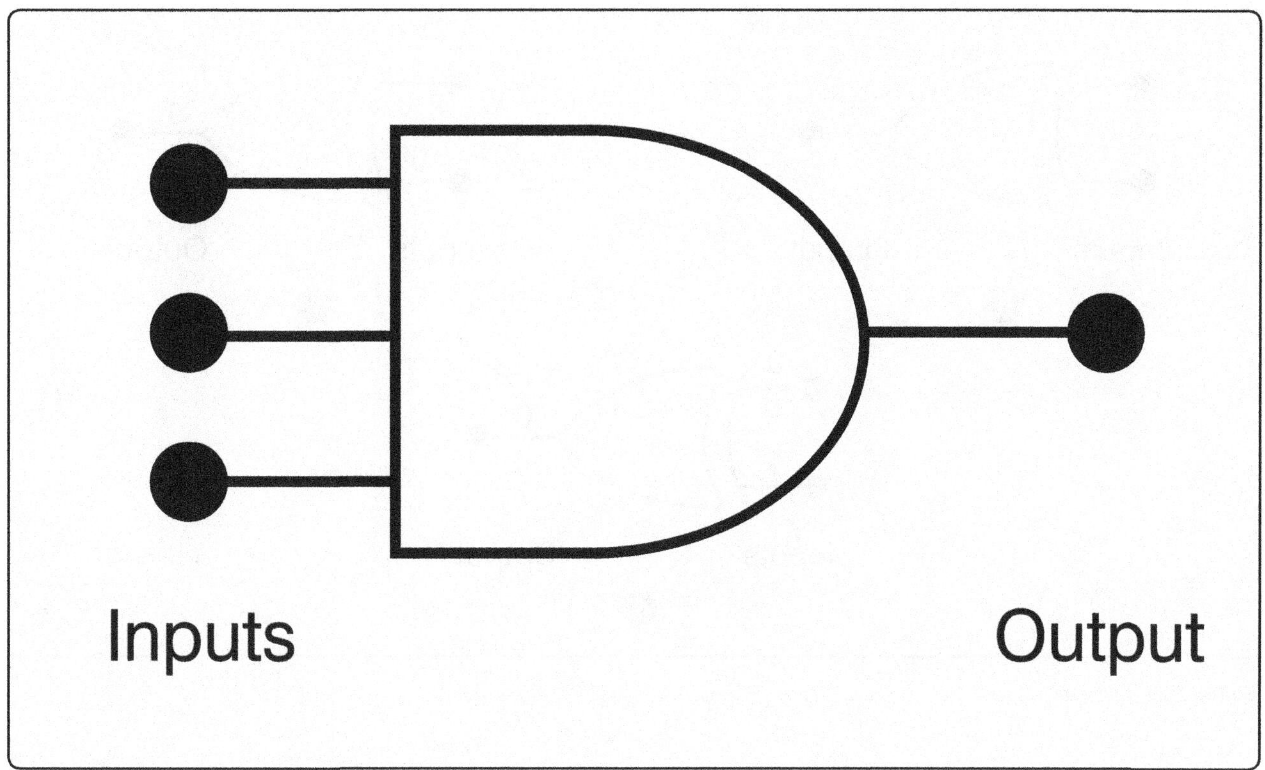

Figure 25. Logic gate.

Appendix 1

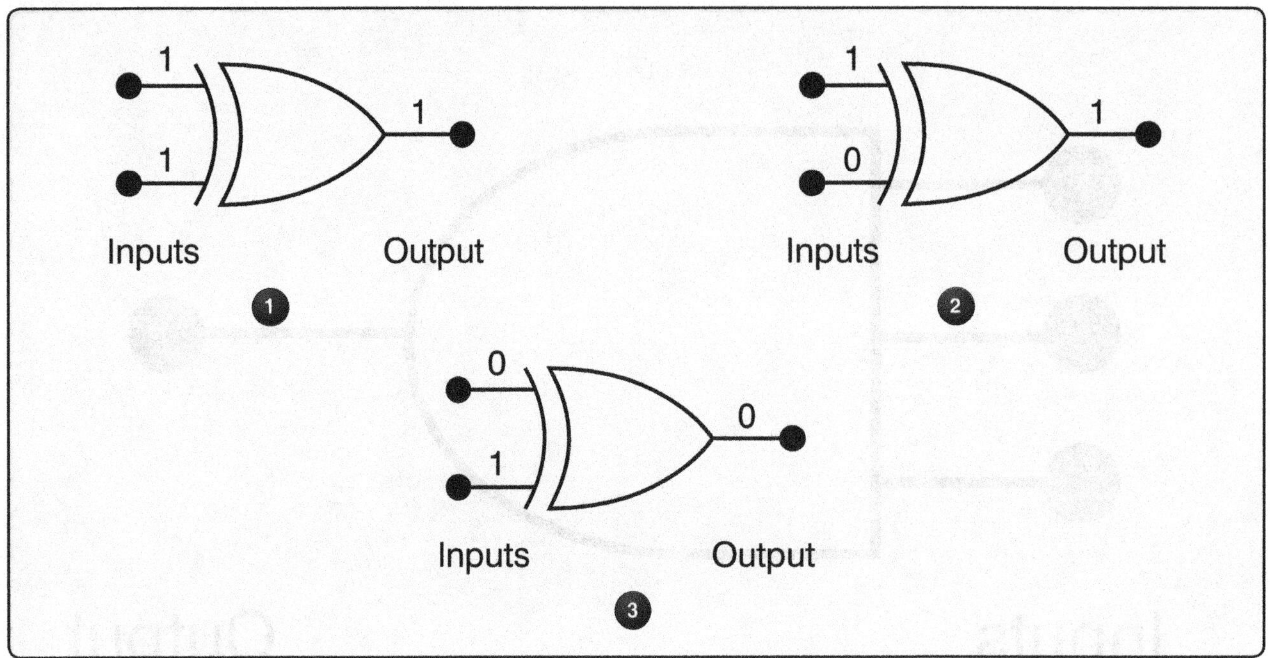

Figure 26. Logic gate.

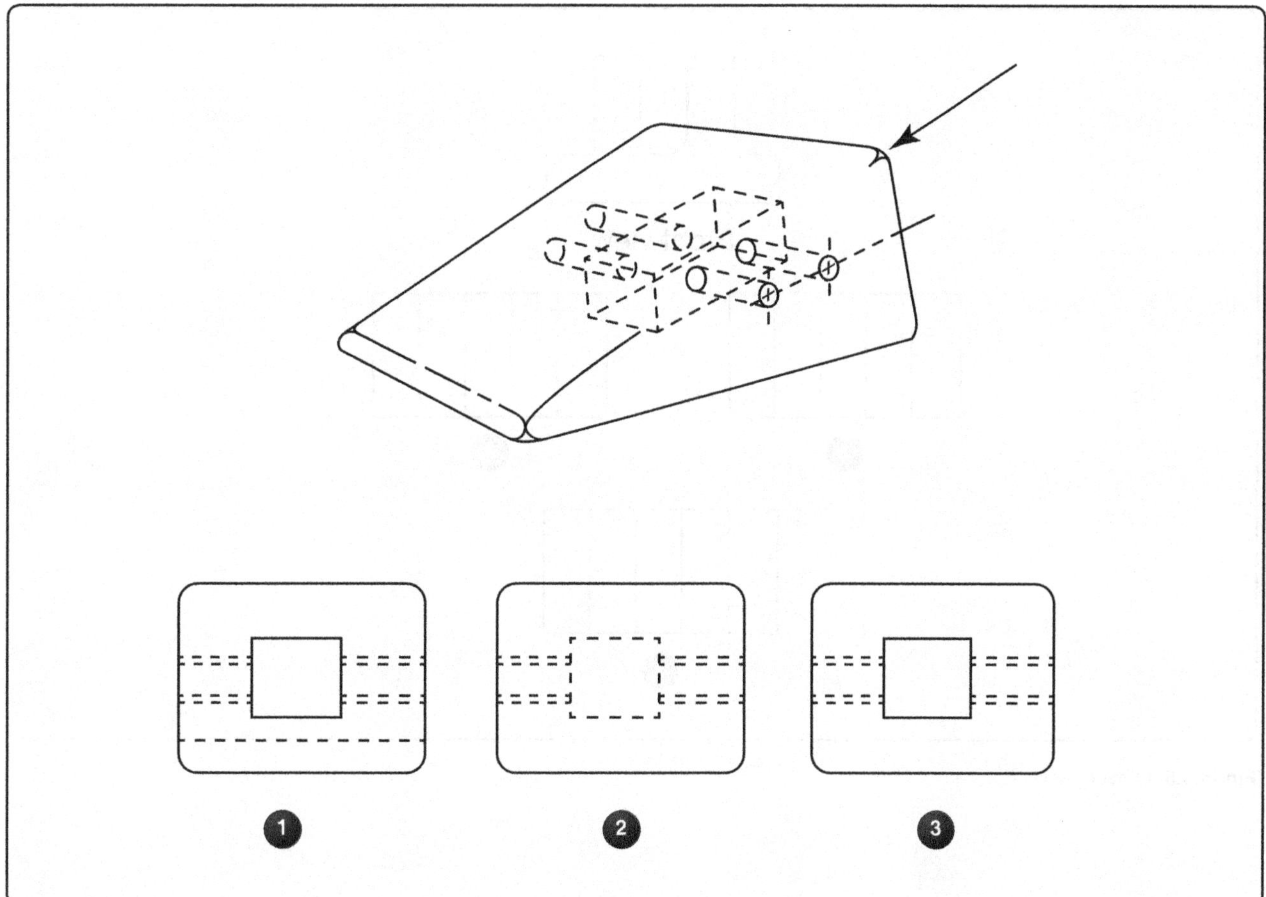

Figure 27. Object views.

Appendix 1

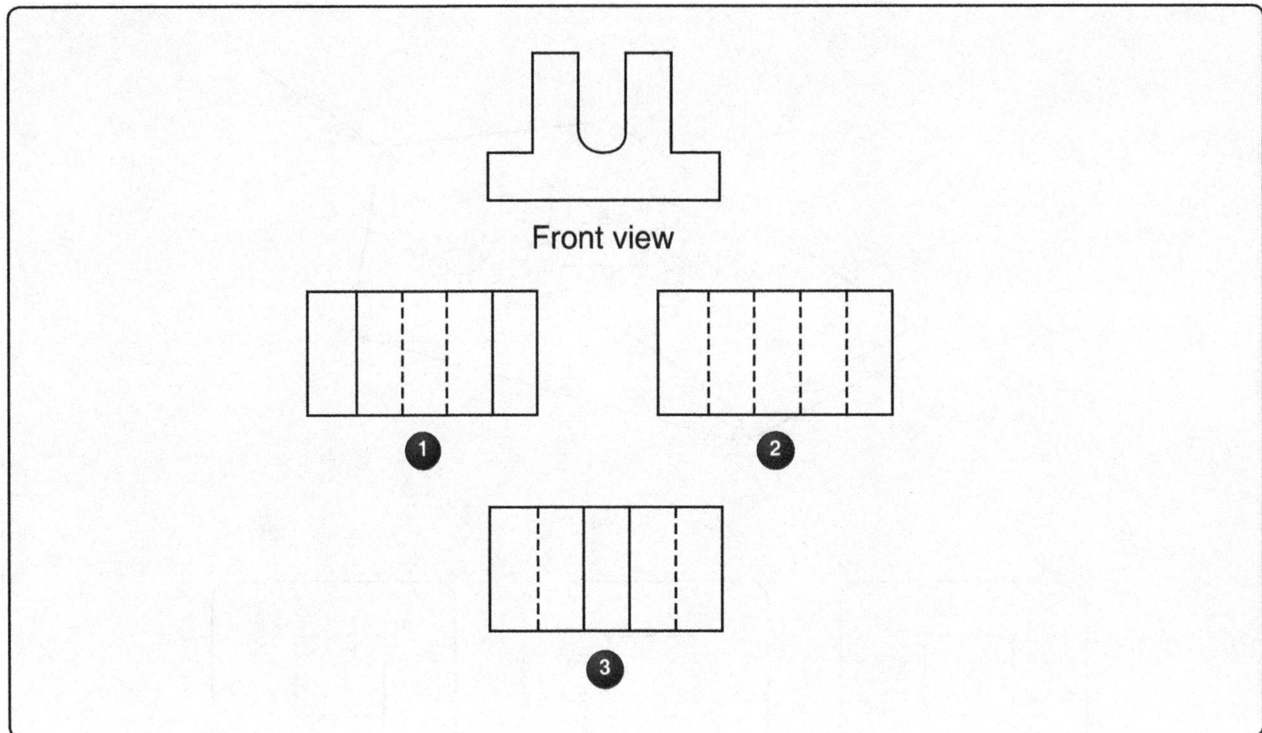

Figure 28. Object views.

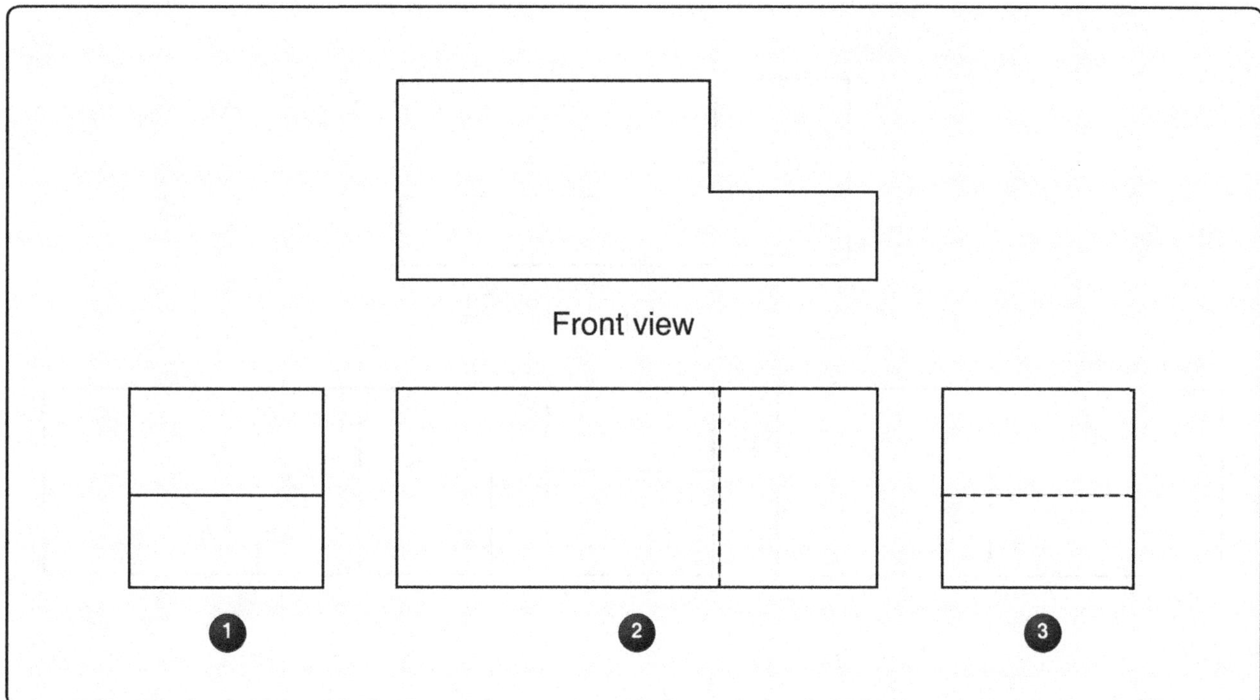

Figure 29. Object views.

Appendix 1

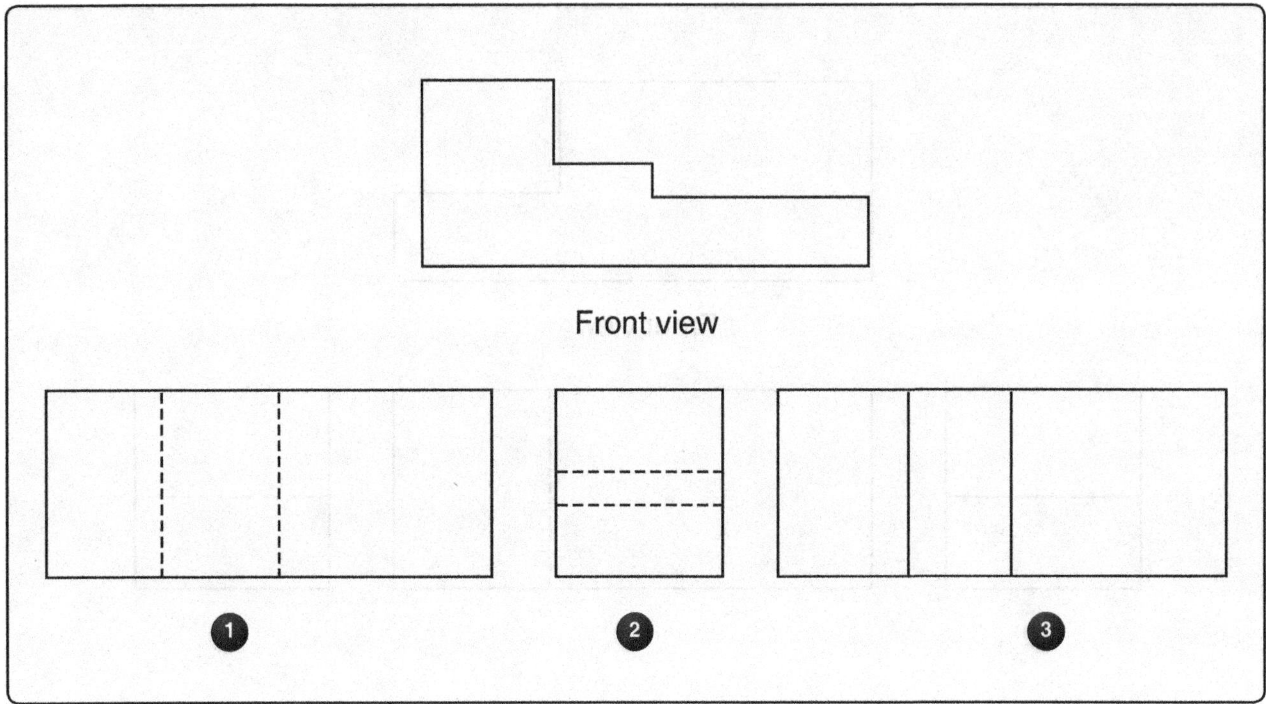

Figure 30. Object views.

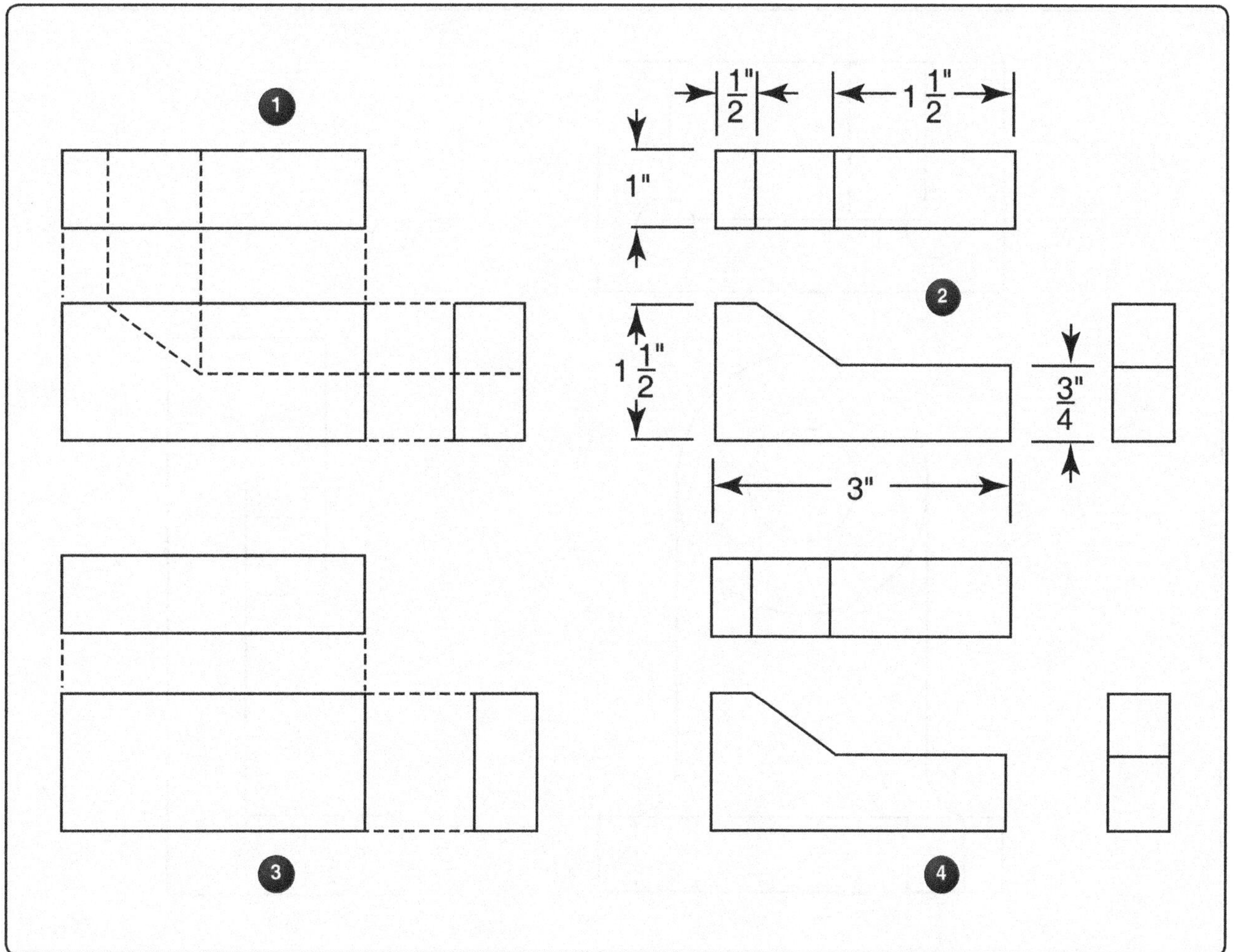

Figure 31. Sketches.

Appendix 1

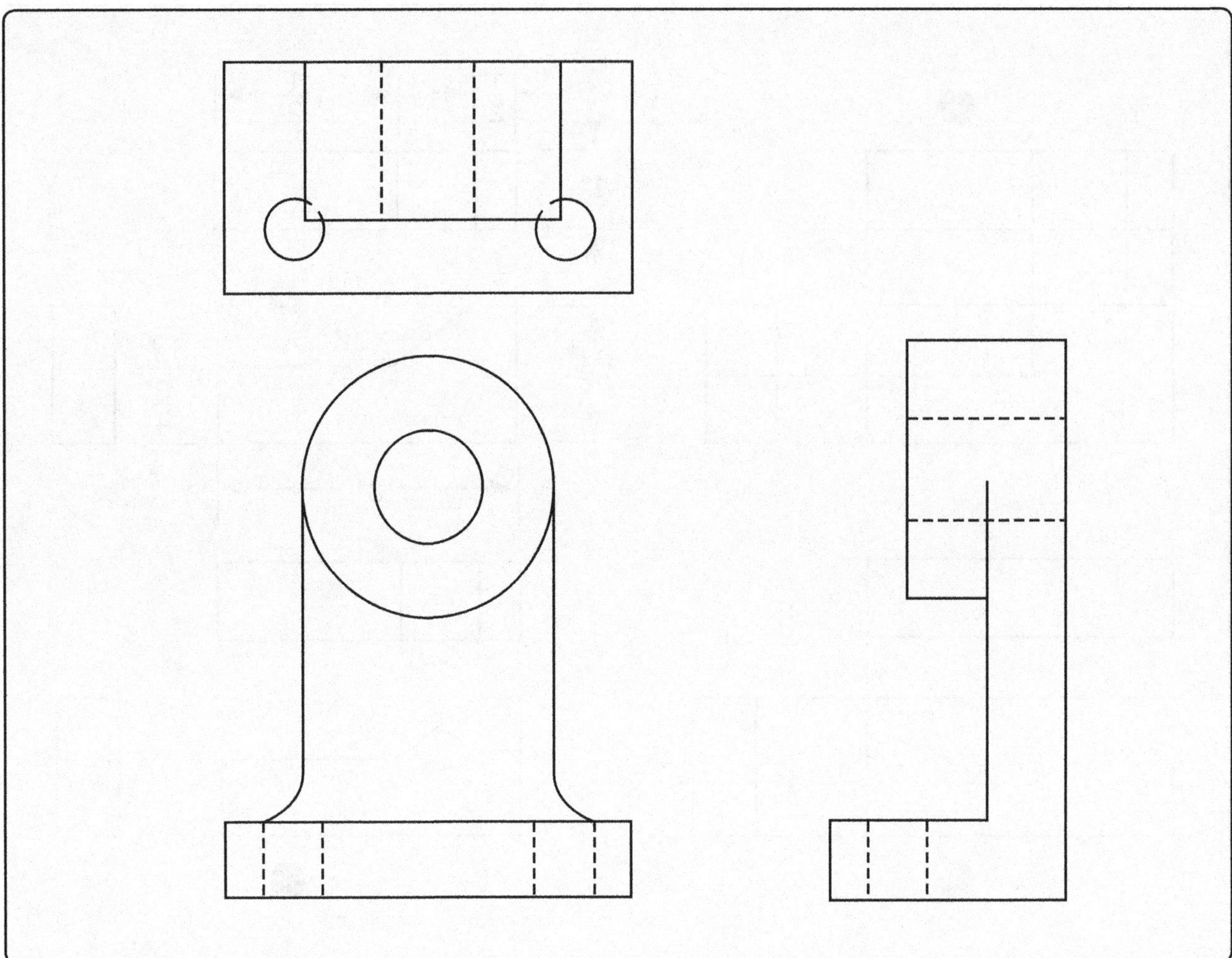

Figure 32. Sketches.

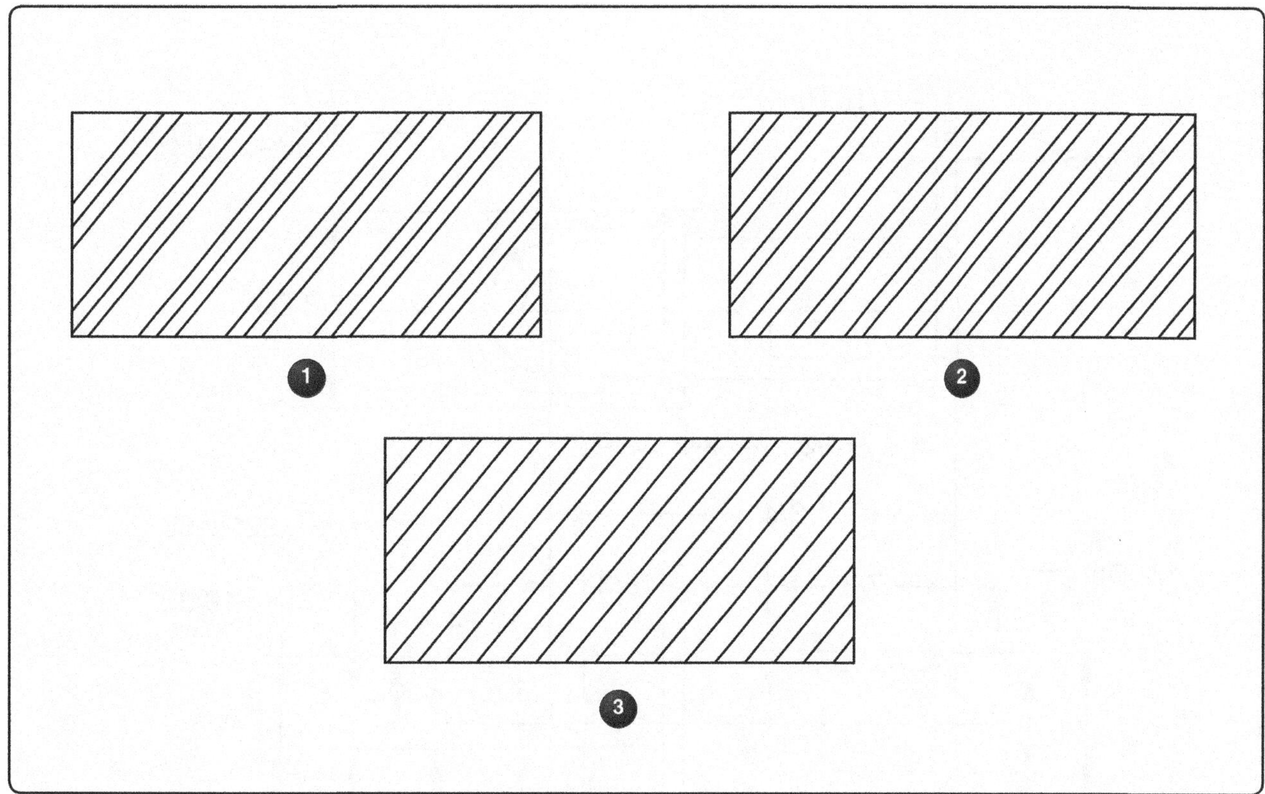

Figure 33. Material symbols.

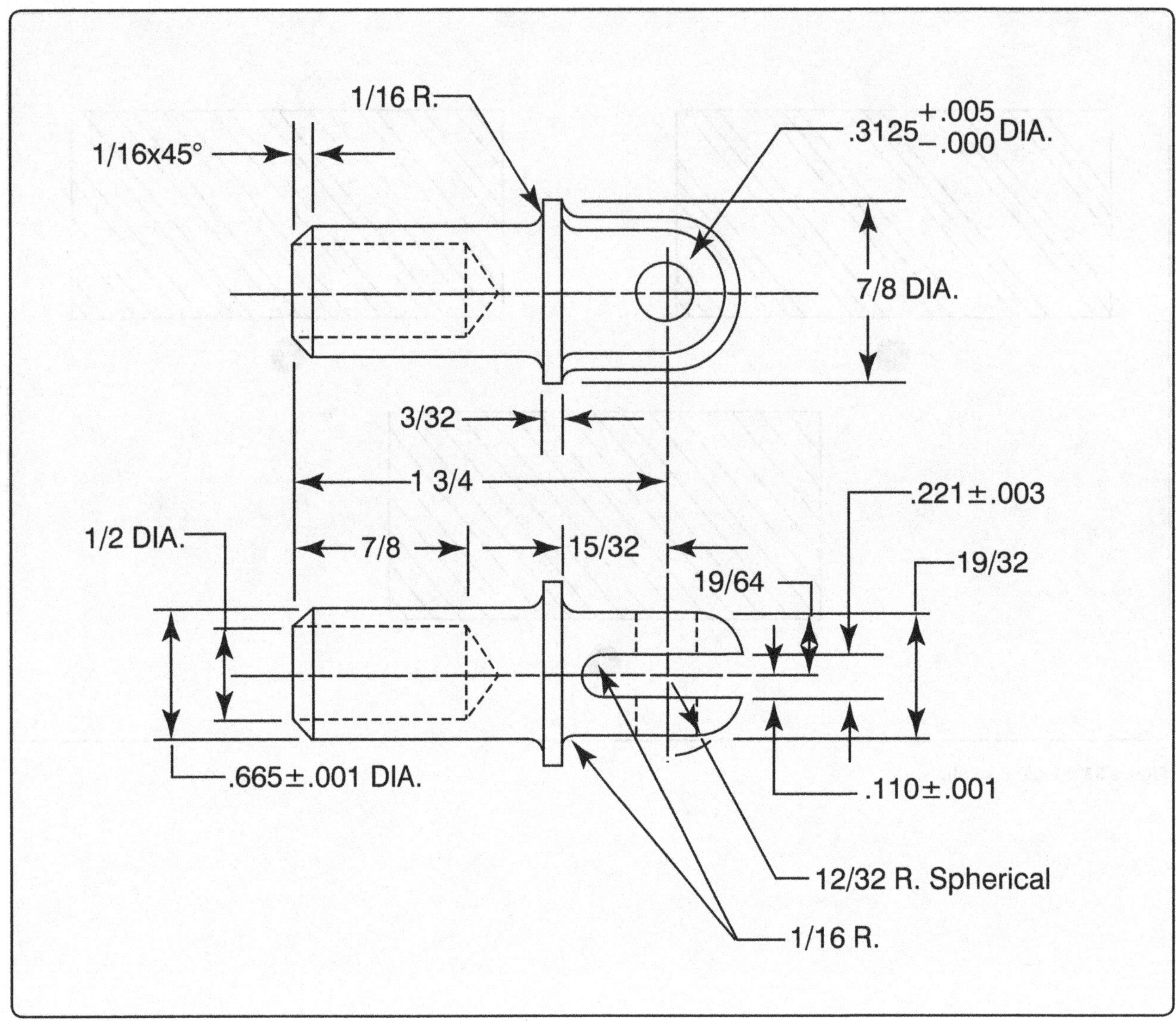

Figure 34. Aircraft drawing.

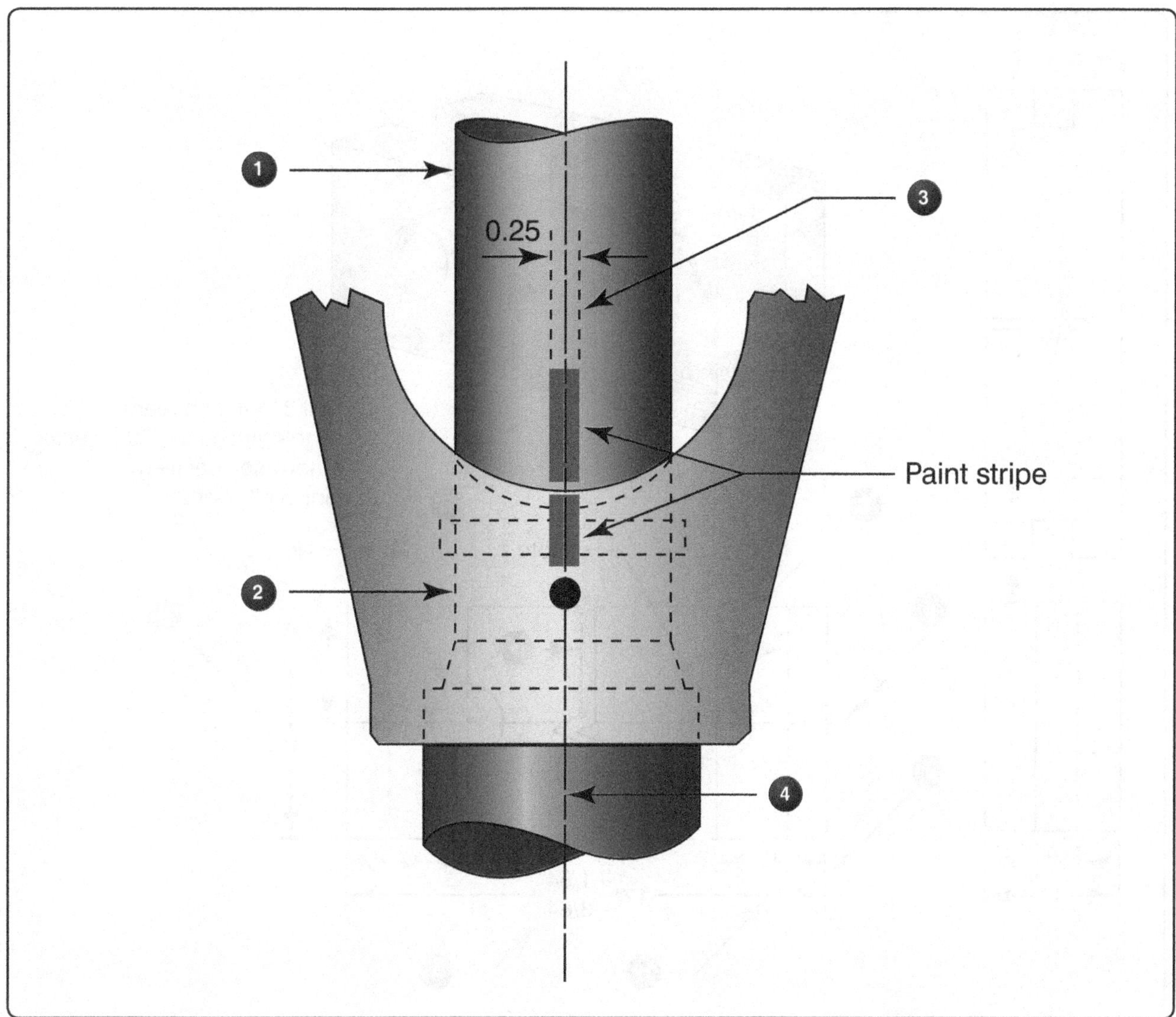

Figure 35. Aircraft drawing.

Appendix 1

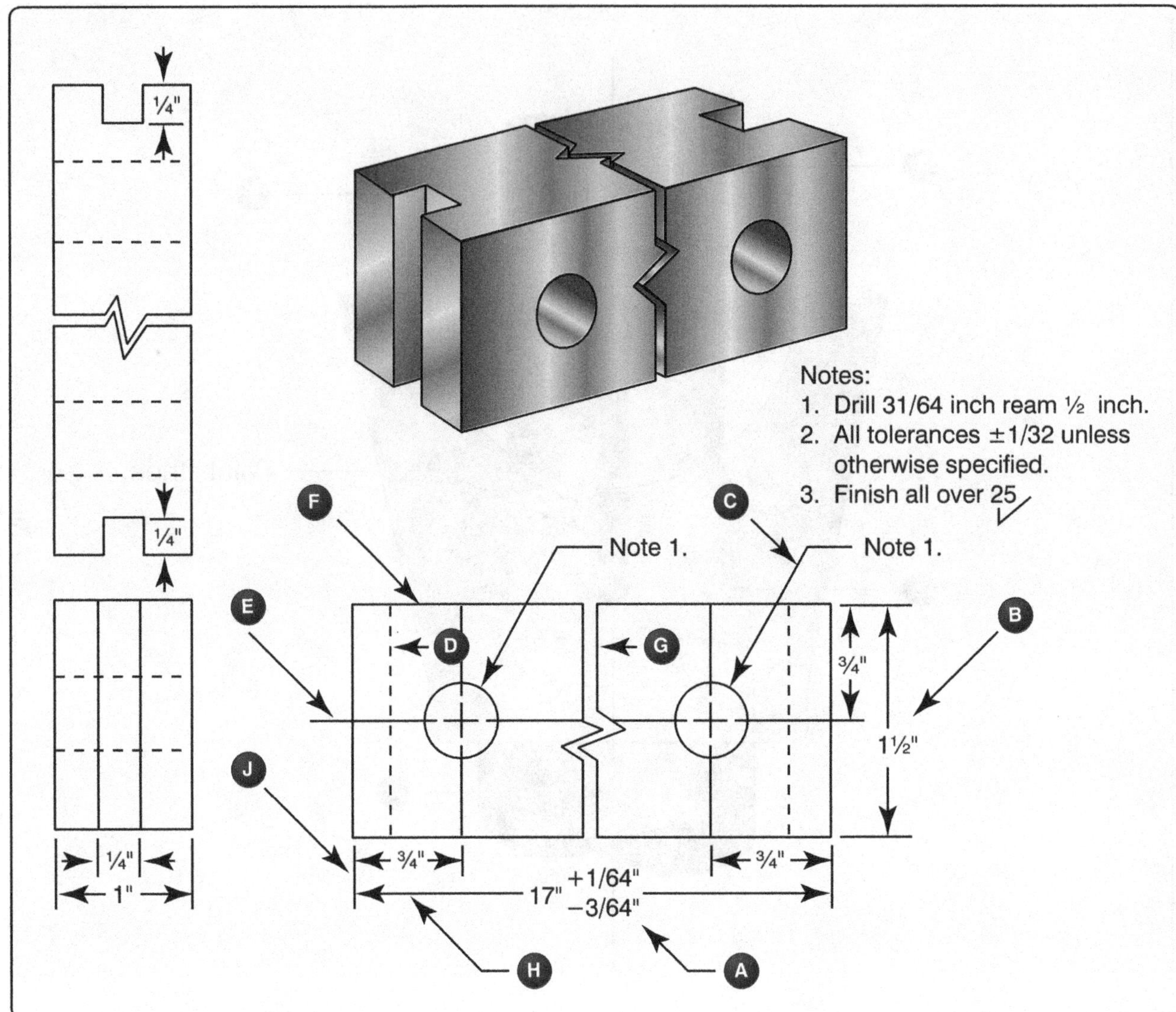

Figure 36. Aircraft drawing.

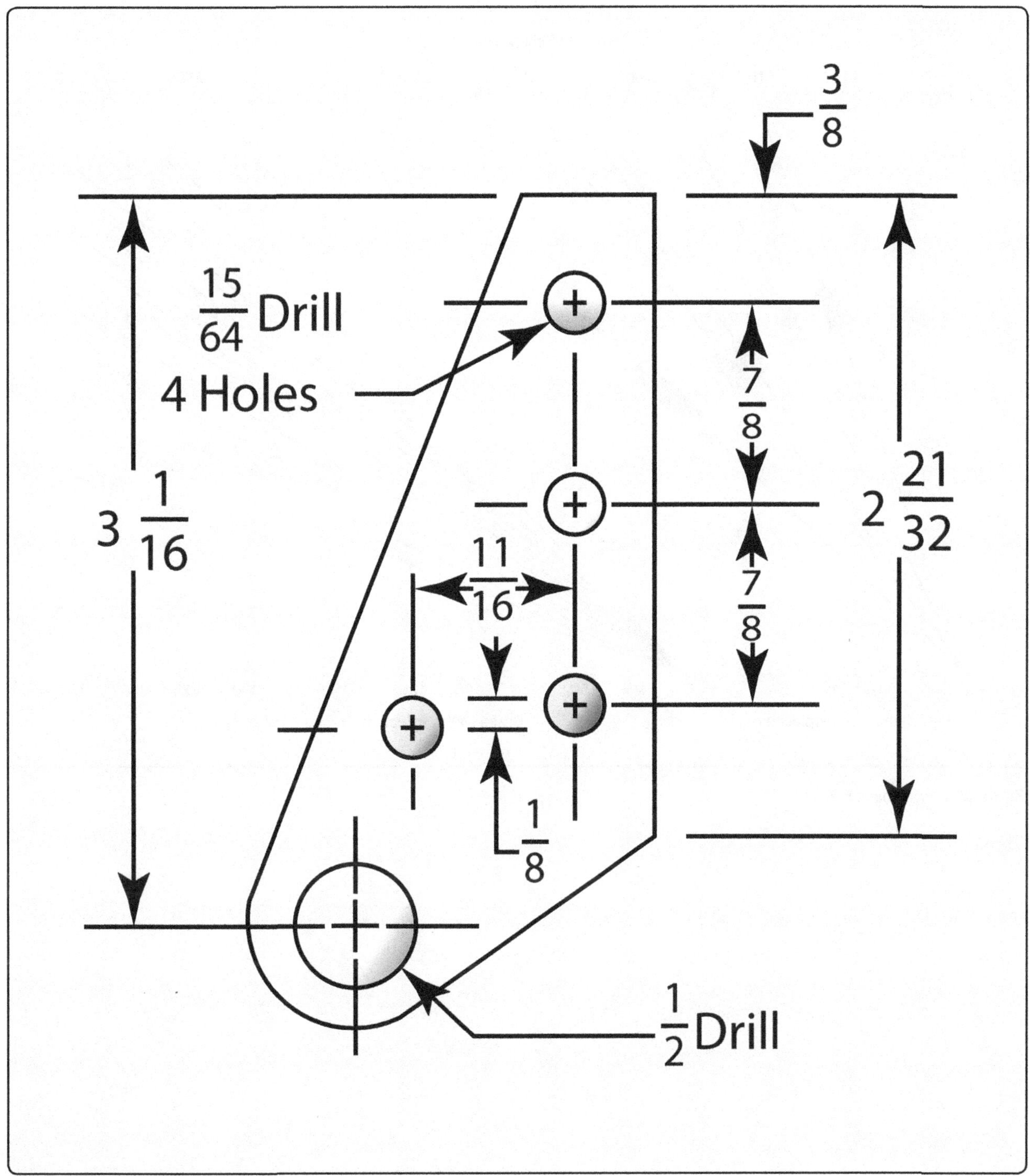

Figure 37. Aircraft drawing.

Appendix 1

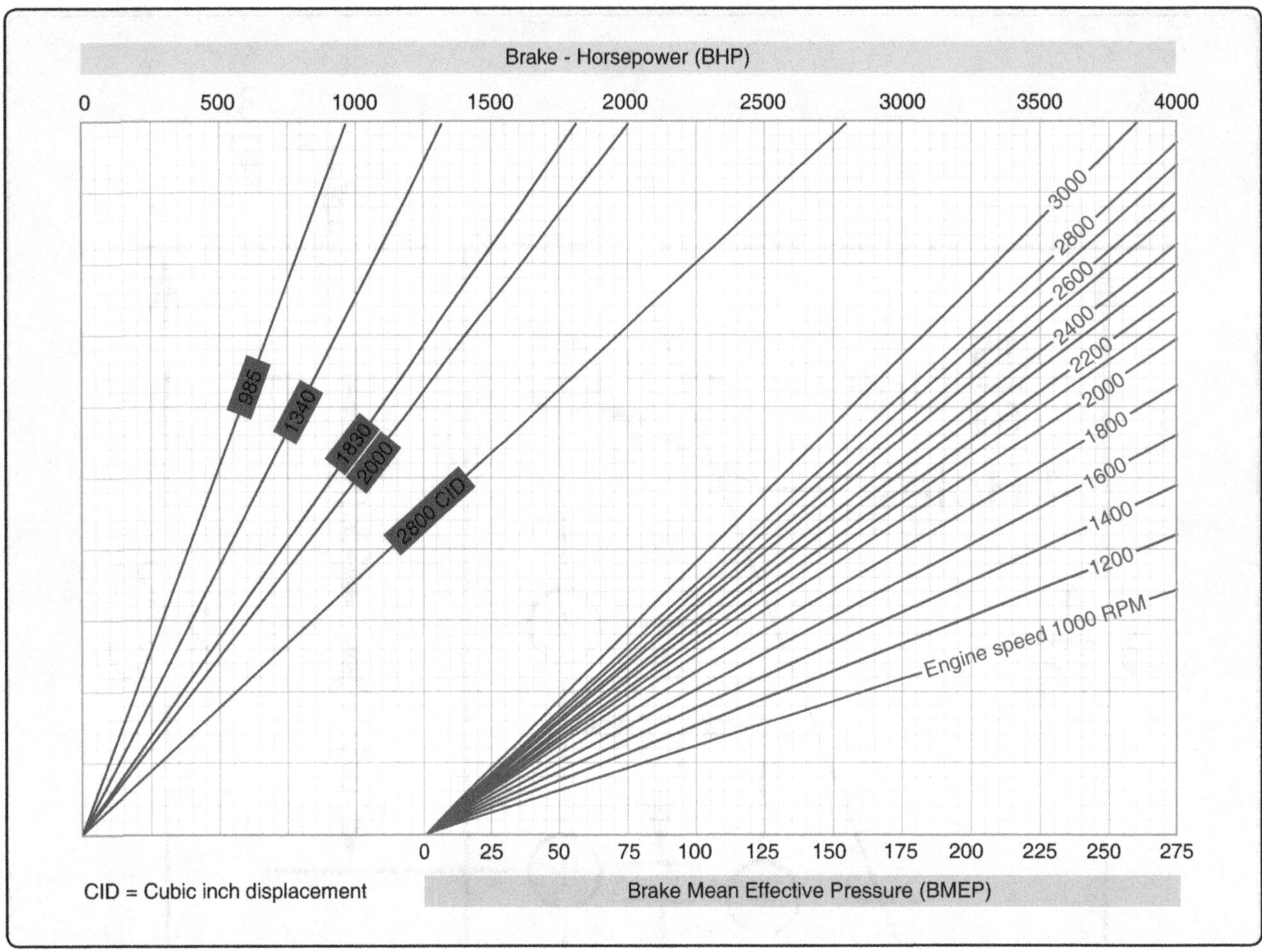

Figure 38. Performance chart.

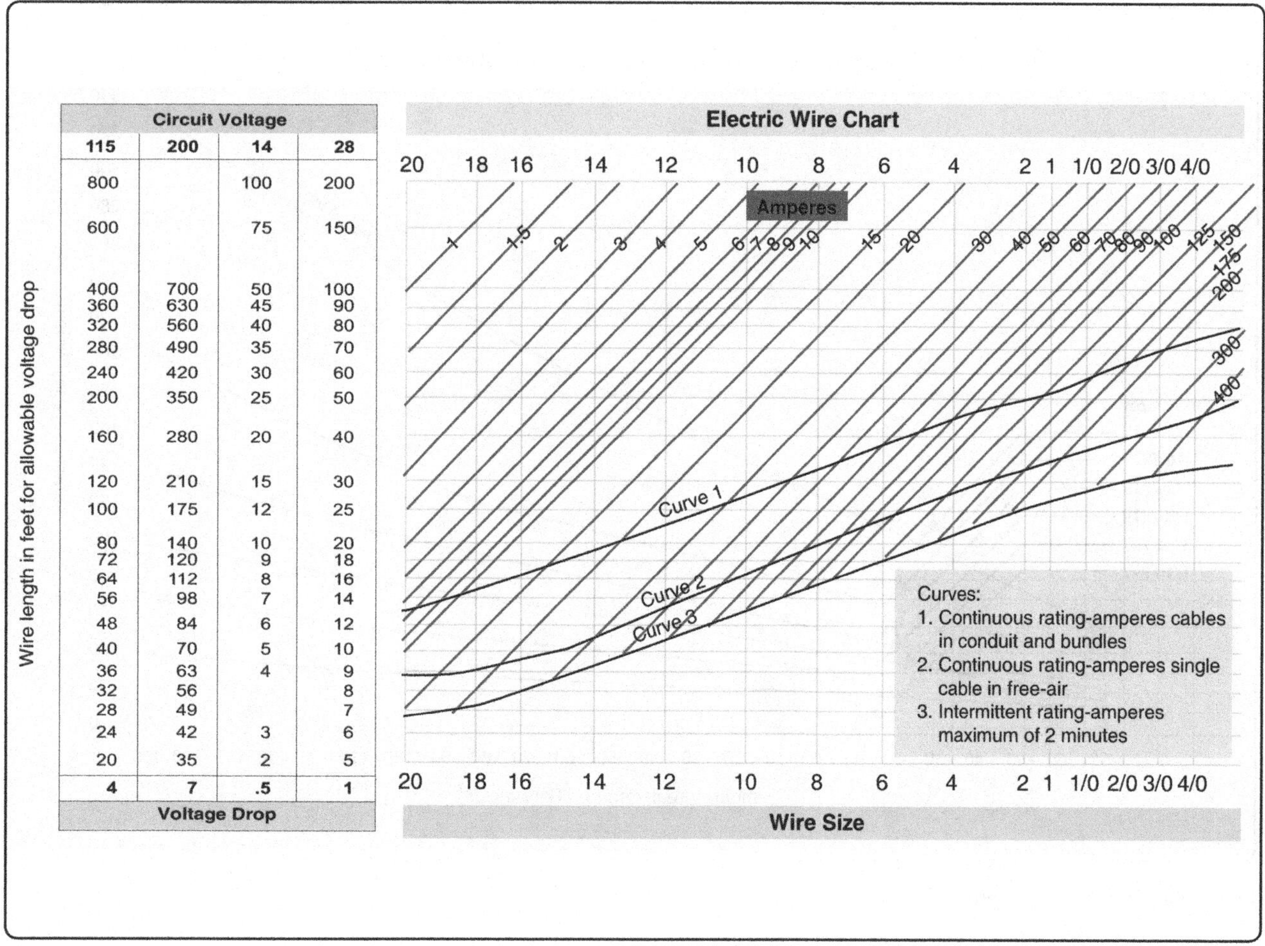

Figure 39. Electric wire chart.

Appendix 1

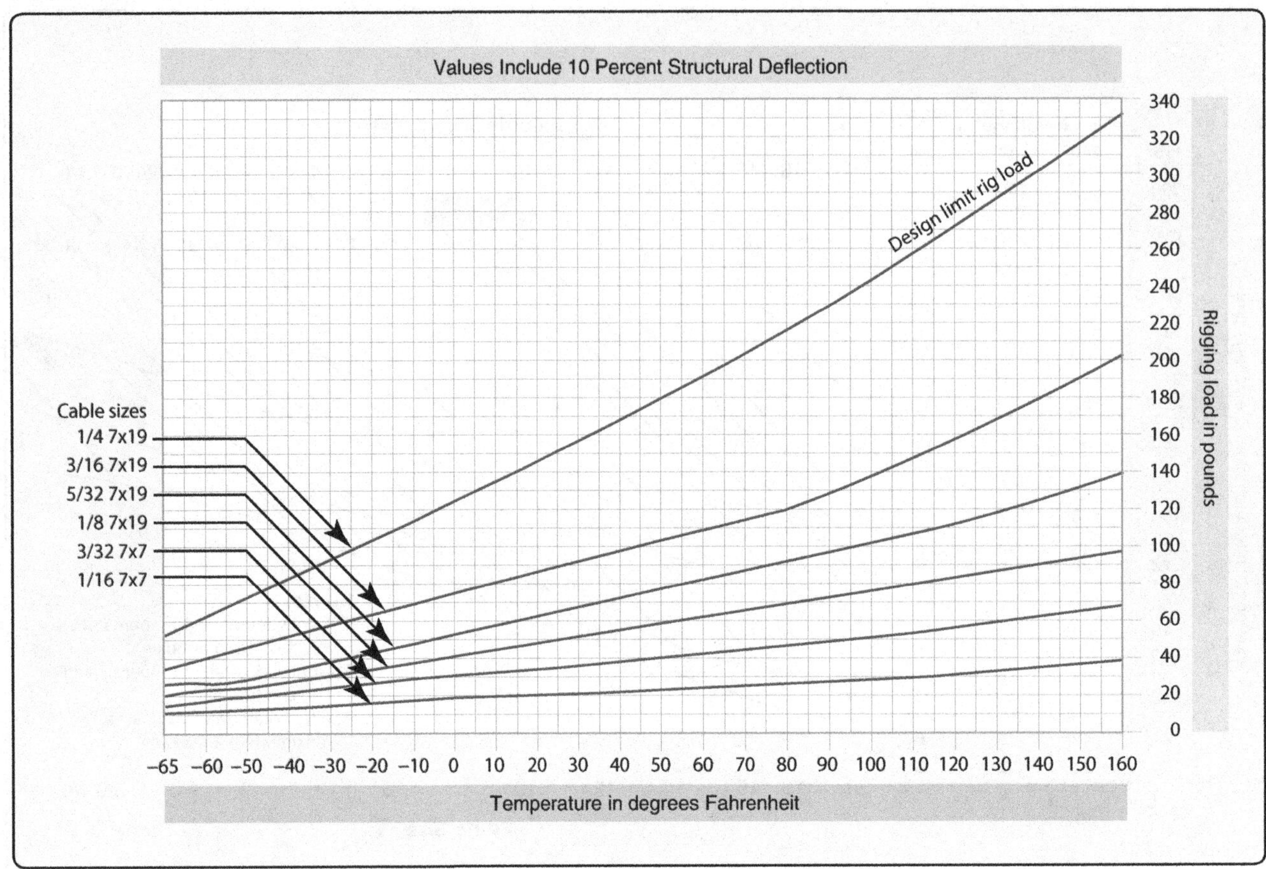

Figure 40. Cable tension chart.

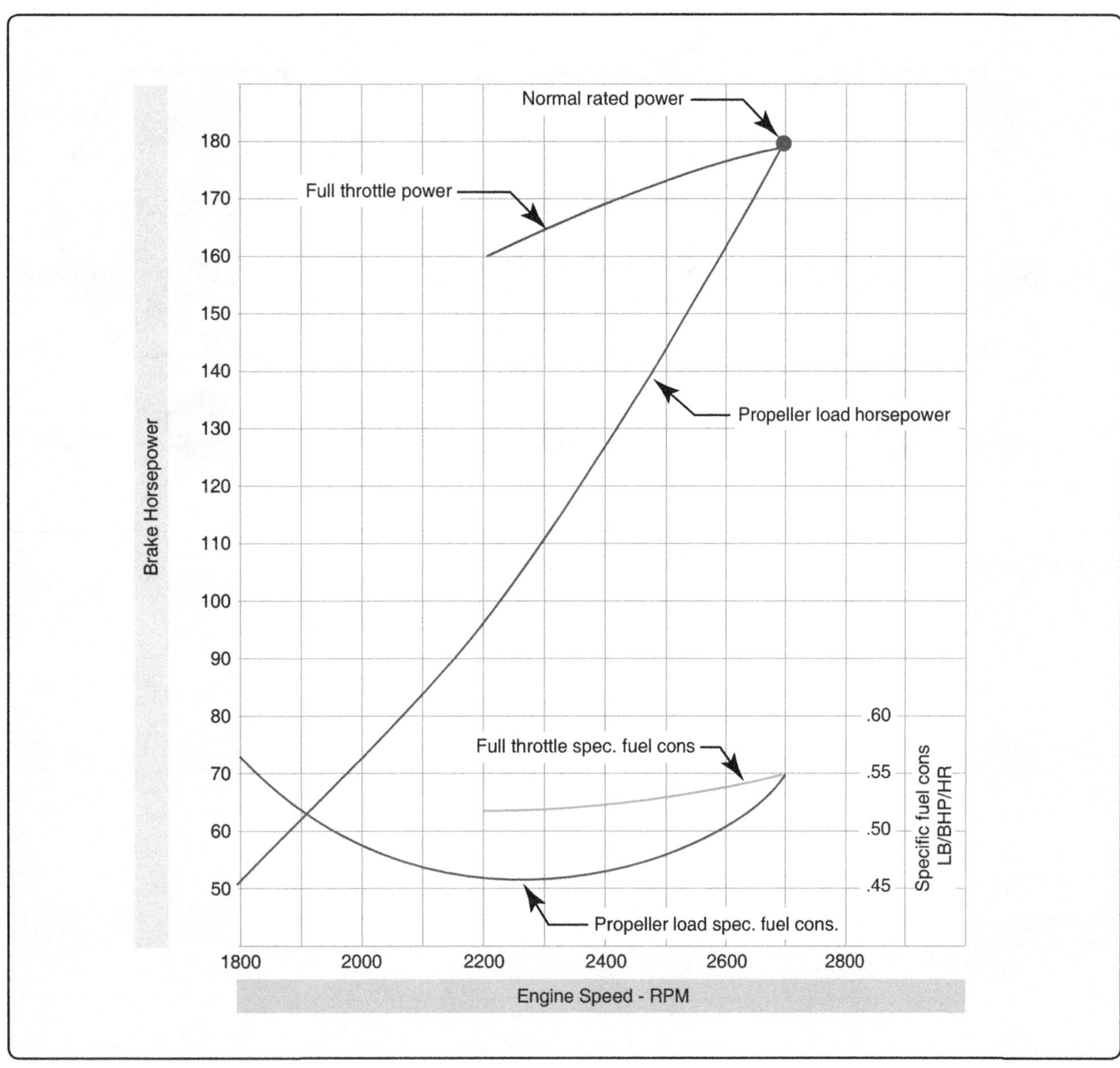

Figure 41. Performance chart.

Appendix 1

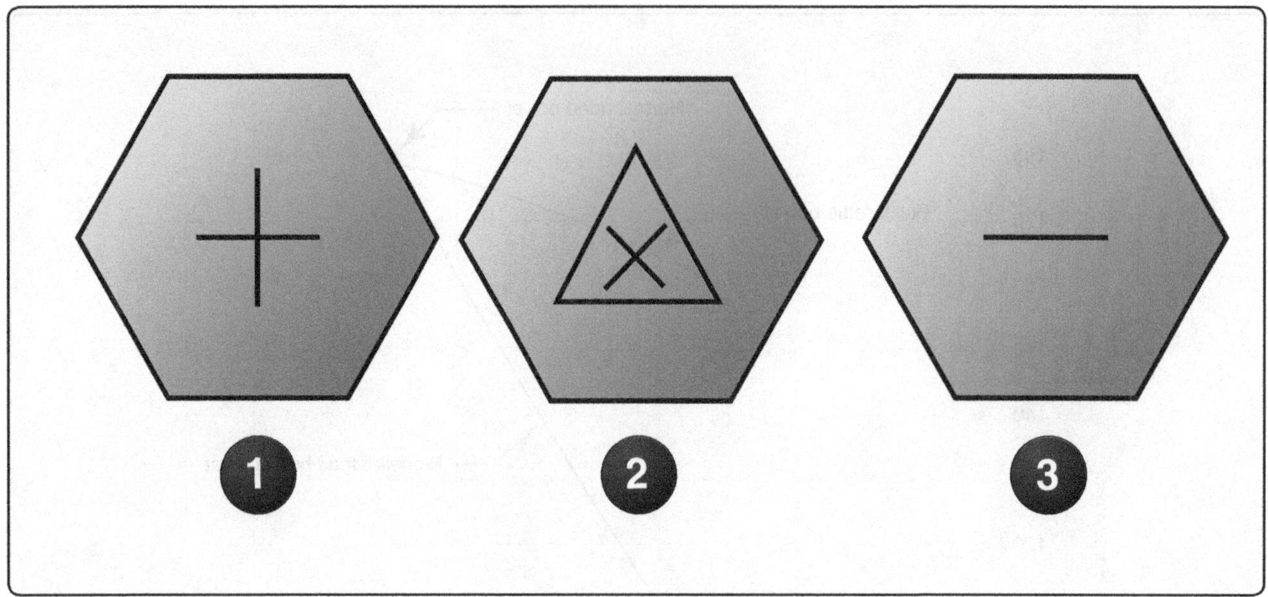

Figure 42. Aircraft hardware.

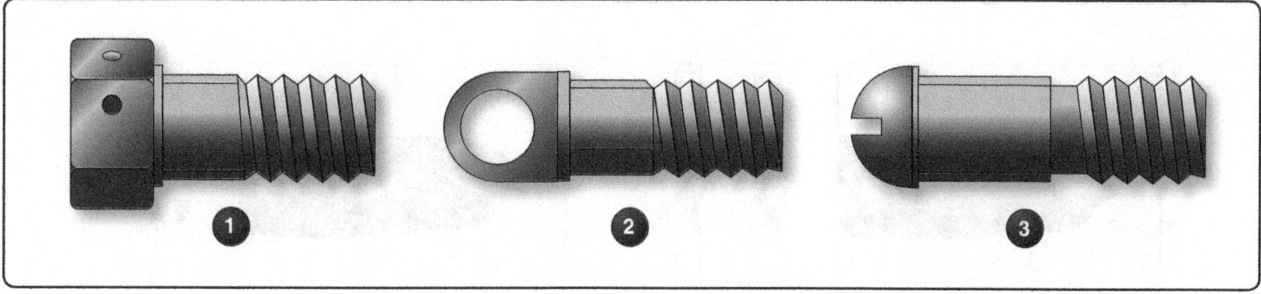

Figure 43. Aircraft hardware.

Appendix 1

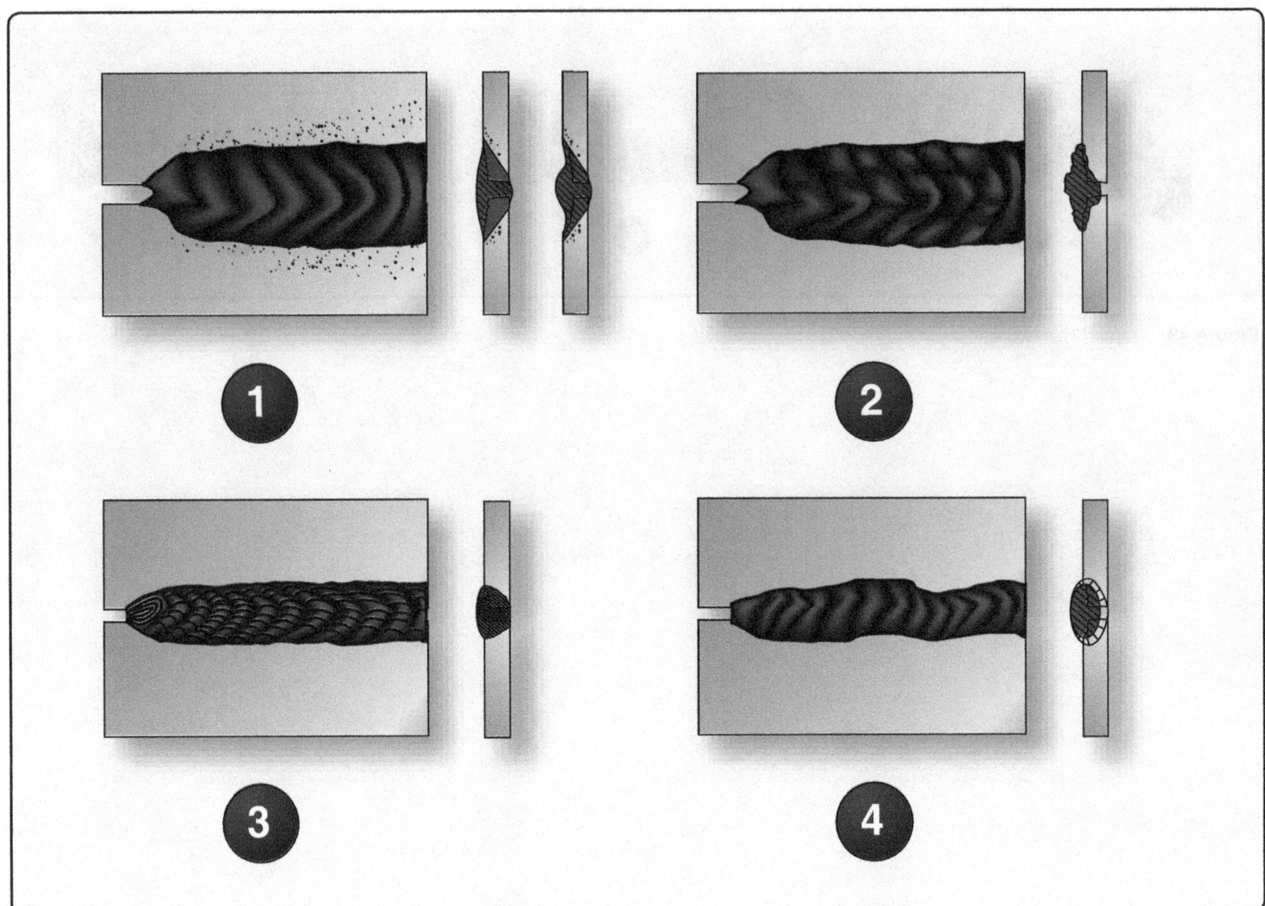

Figure 44. Welds.

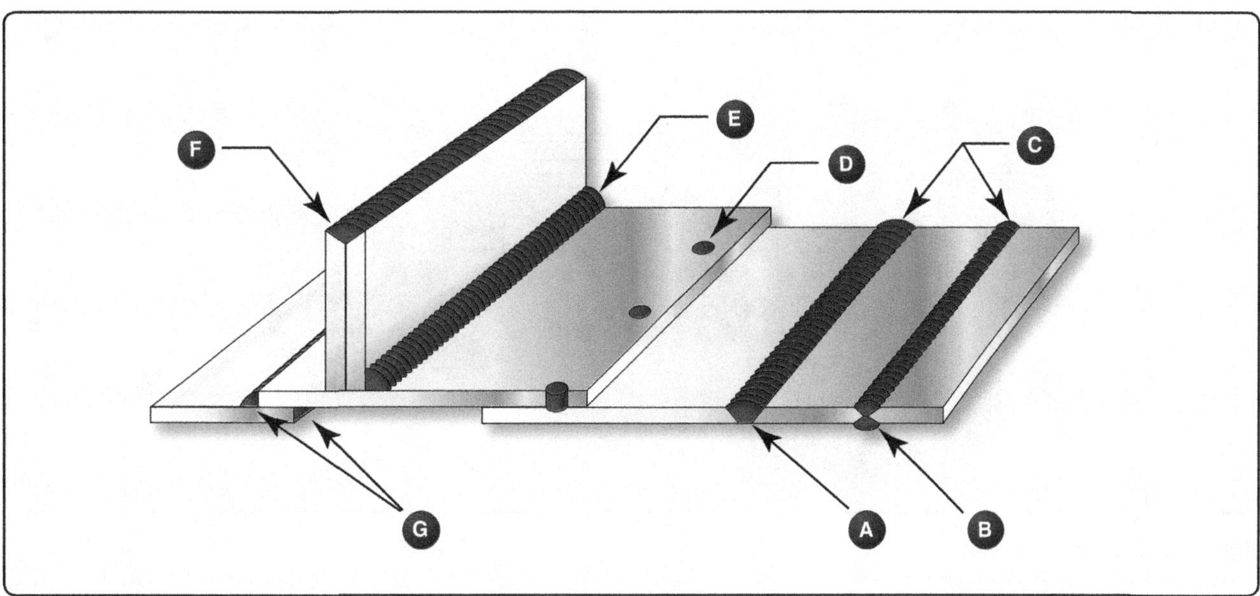

Figure 45. Welds.

Appendix 1

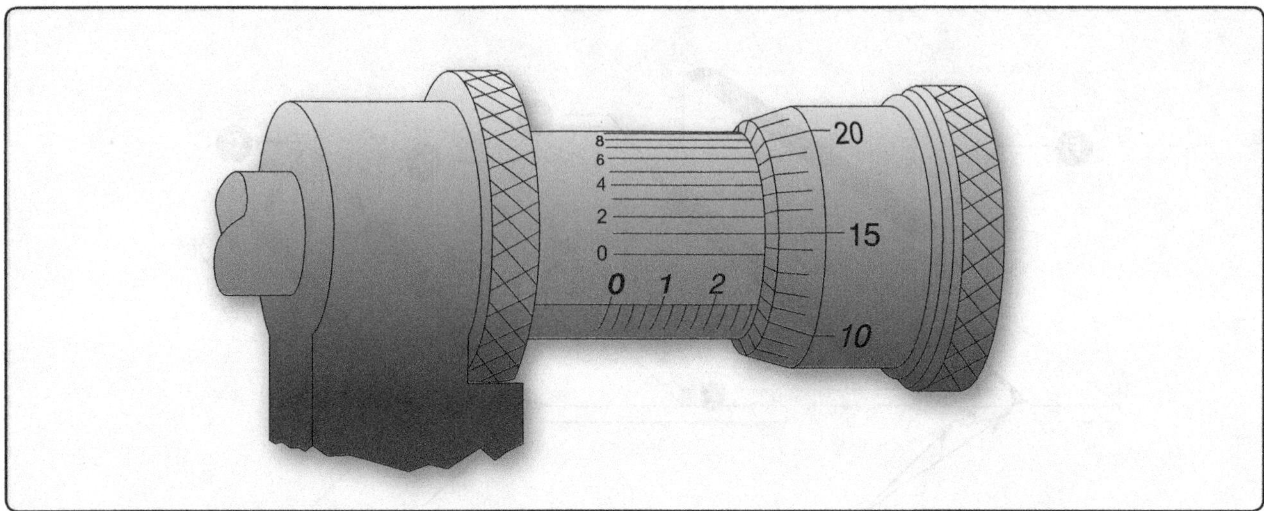

Figure 46. Precision measurement.

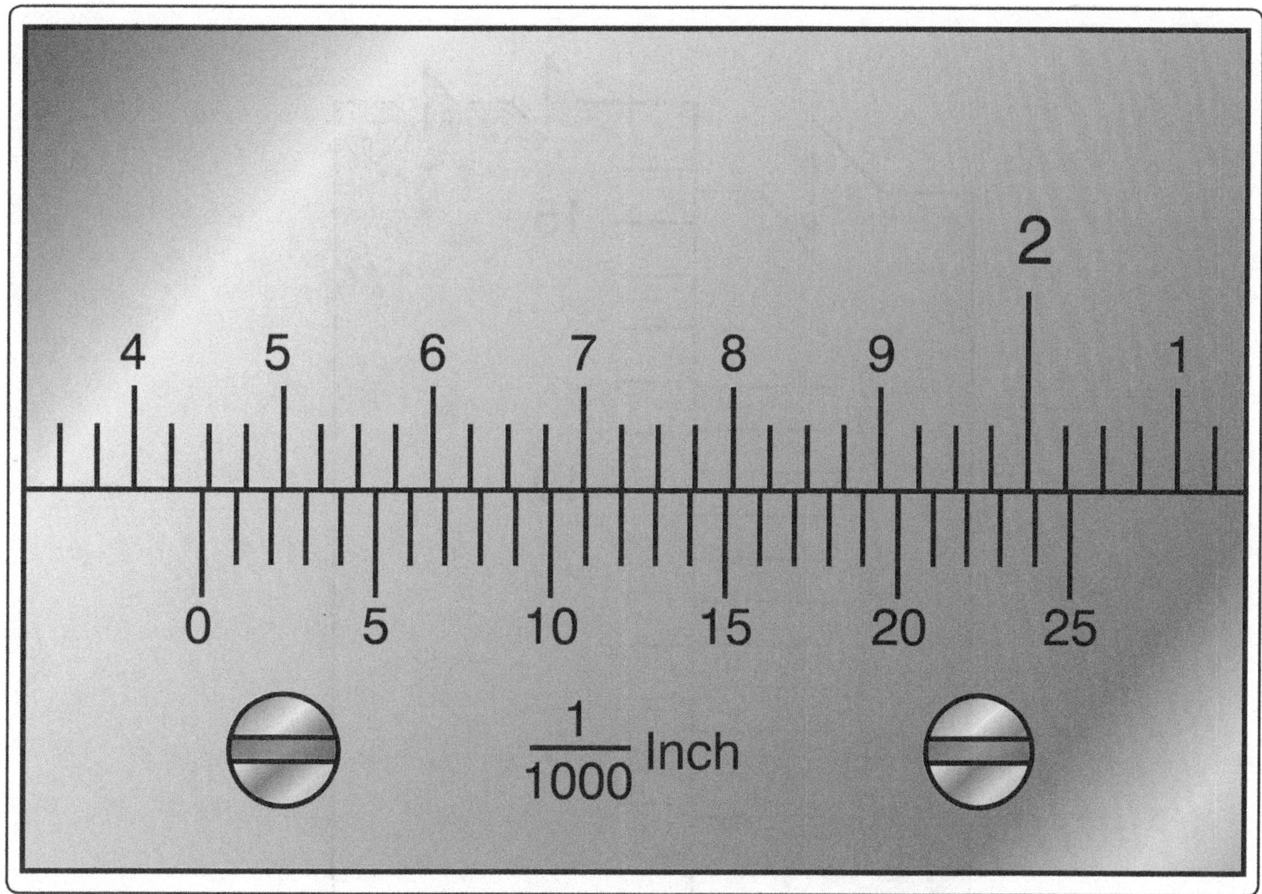

Figure 47. Precision measurement.

Appendix 1

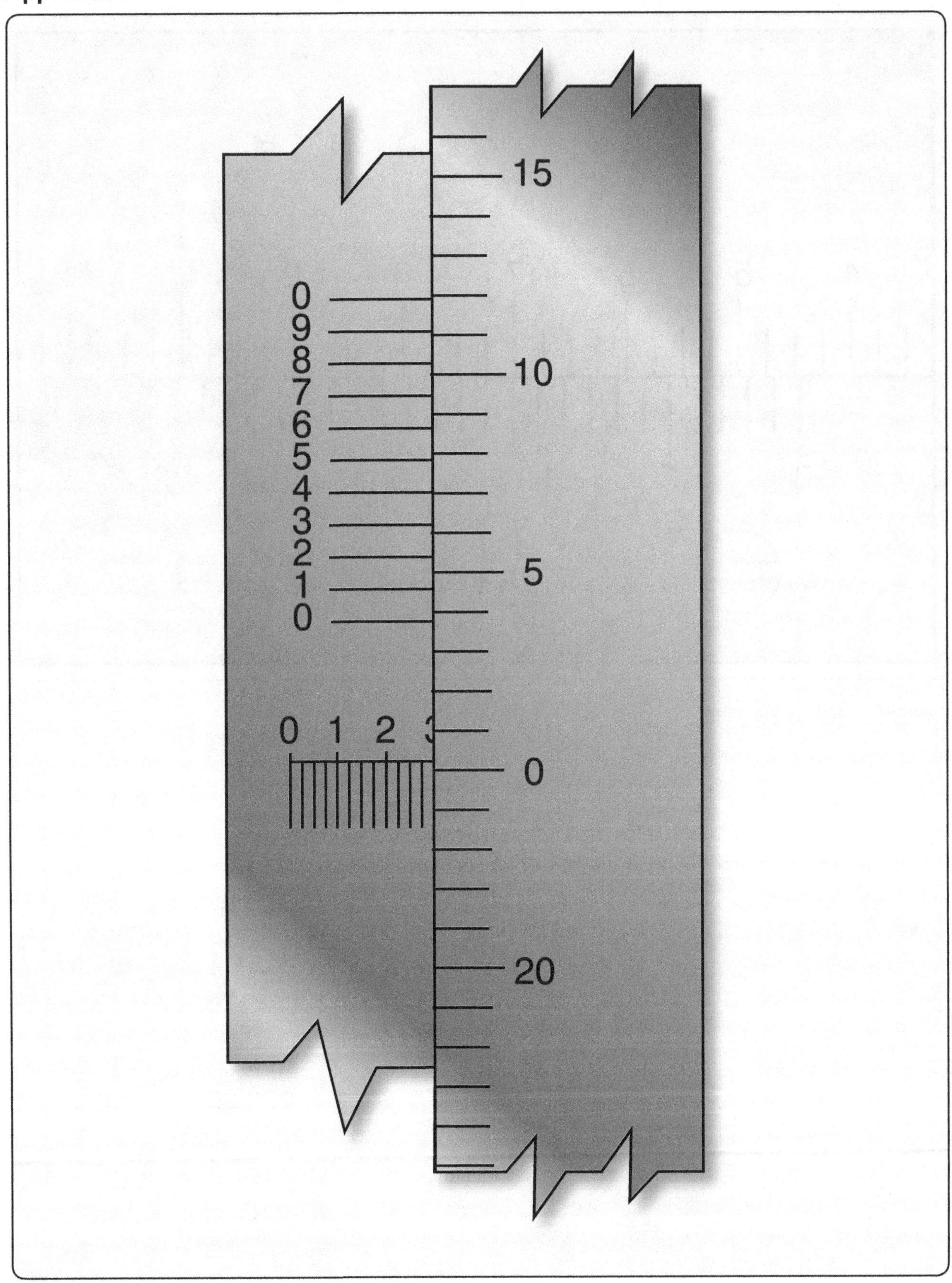

Figure 48. Precision measurement.

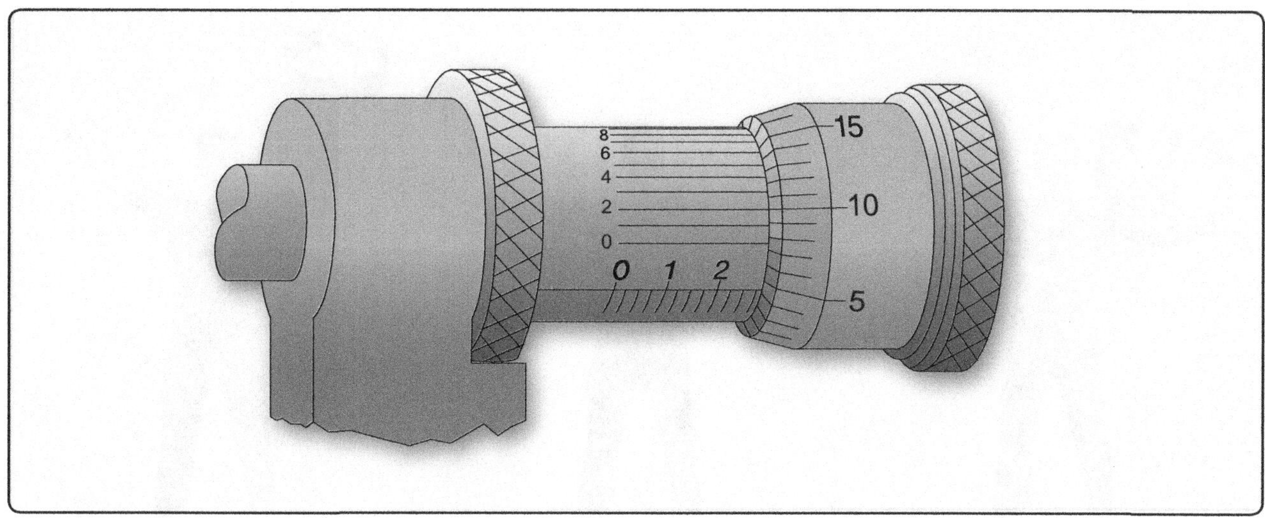

Figure 49. Precision measurement.

Figure 50. Marshalling signals.

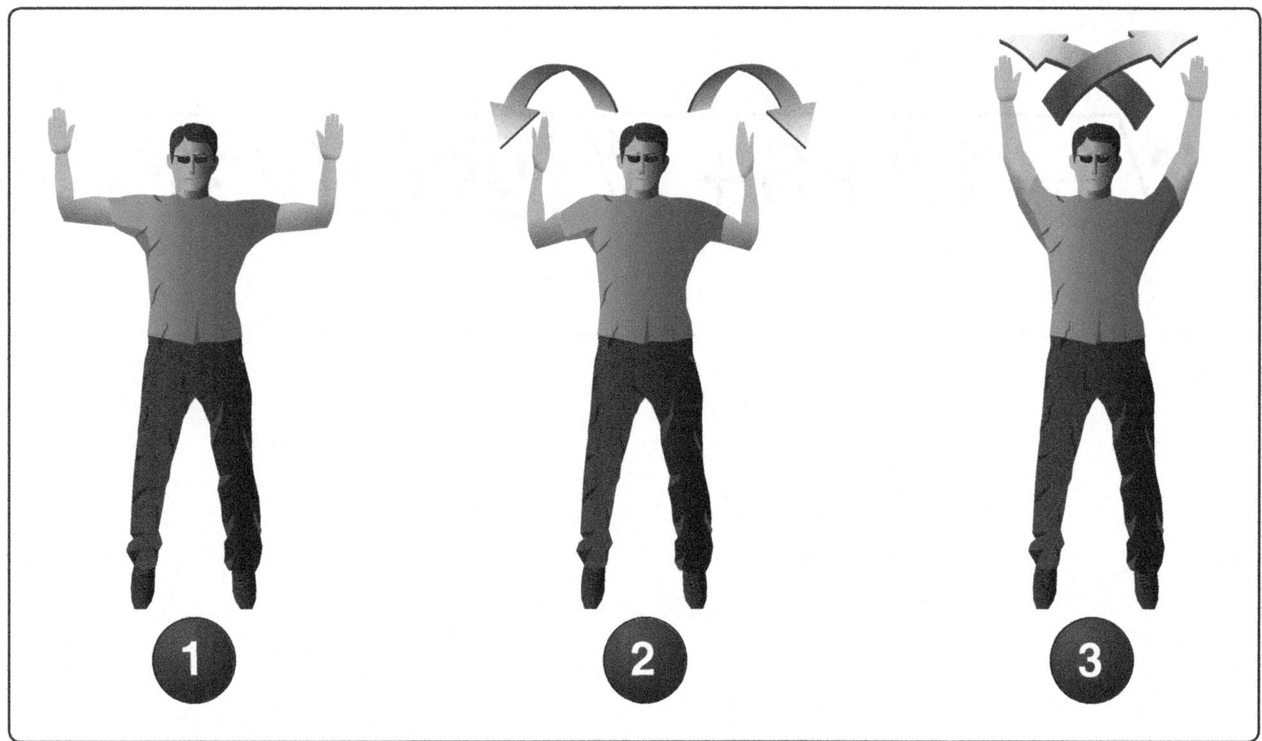

Figure 51. Marshalling signals.

Appendix 1

$$(\sqrt{(-4)^0+6+(\sqrt[4]{1296})(\sqrt{3})^2}=$$

Figure 52. Equation.

$$\frac{\sqrt[2]{31} + \sqrt[2]{43}}{(17)^2} =$$

Figure 53. Equation.

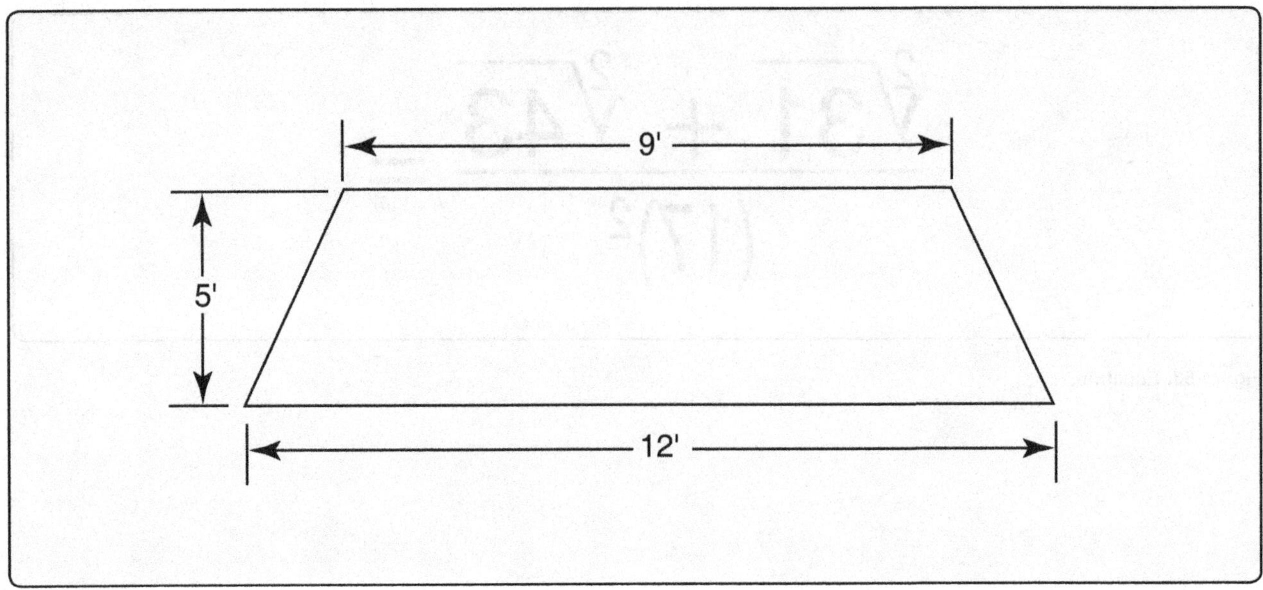

Figure 54. Trapezoid area.

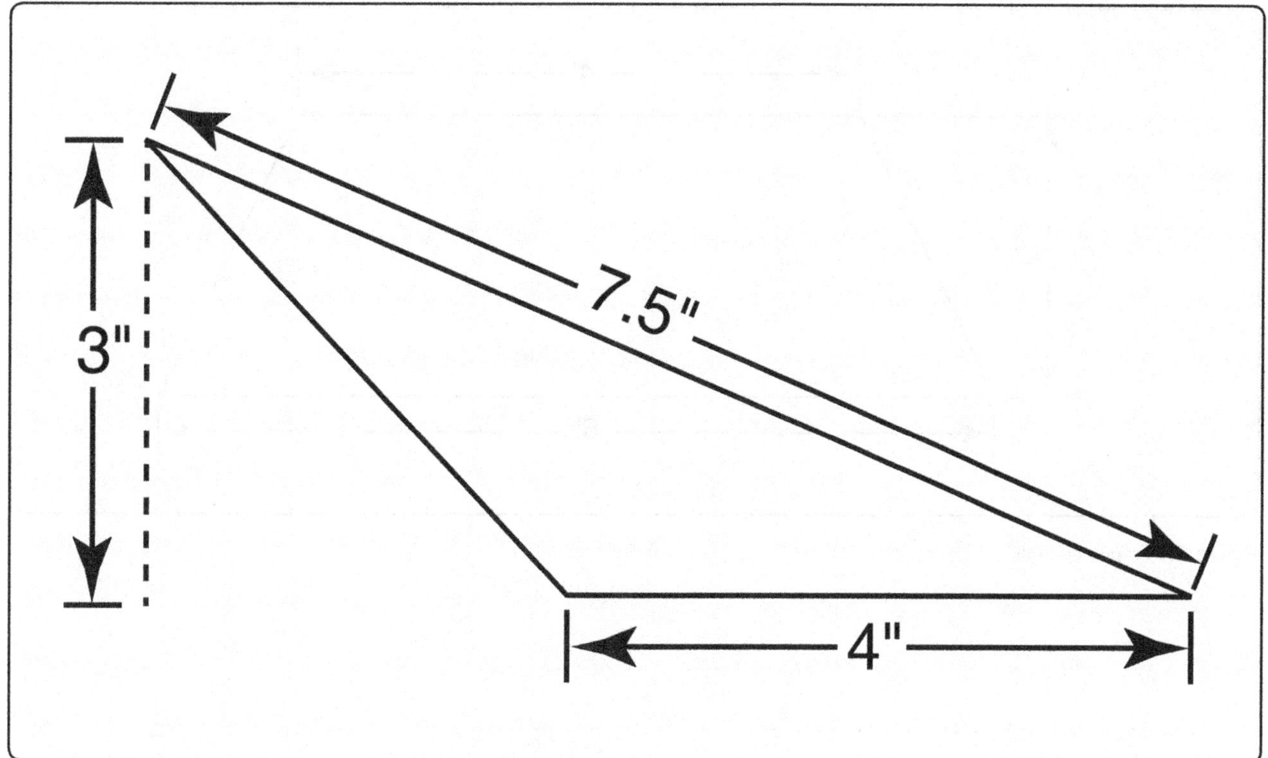

Figure 55. Triangle area.

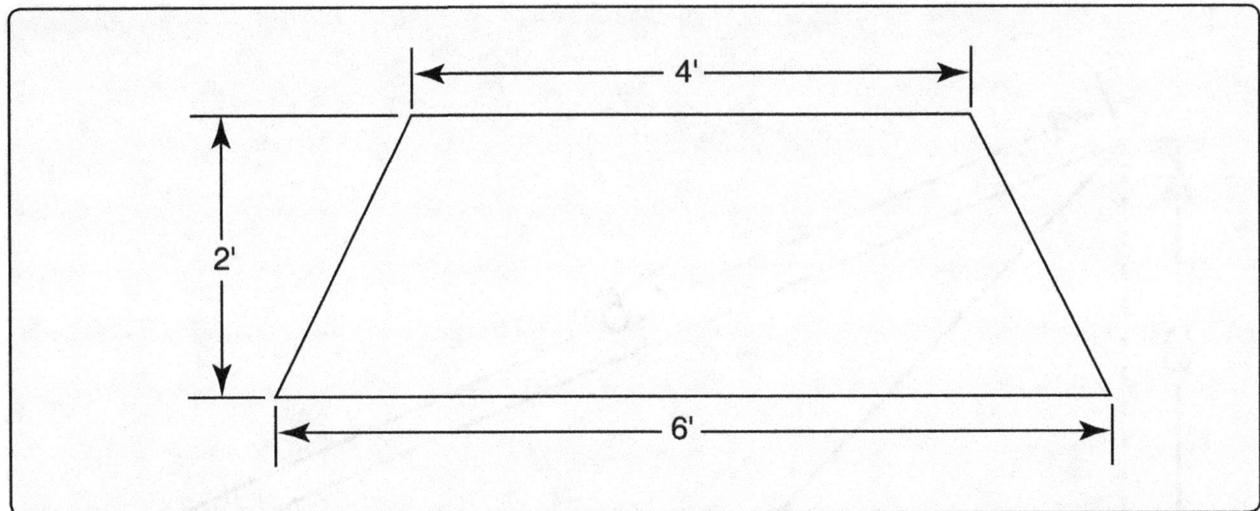

Figure 56. Trapezoid area.

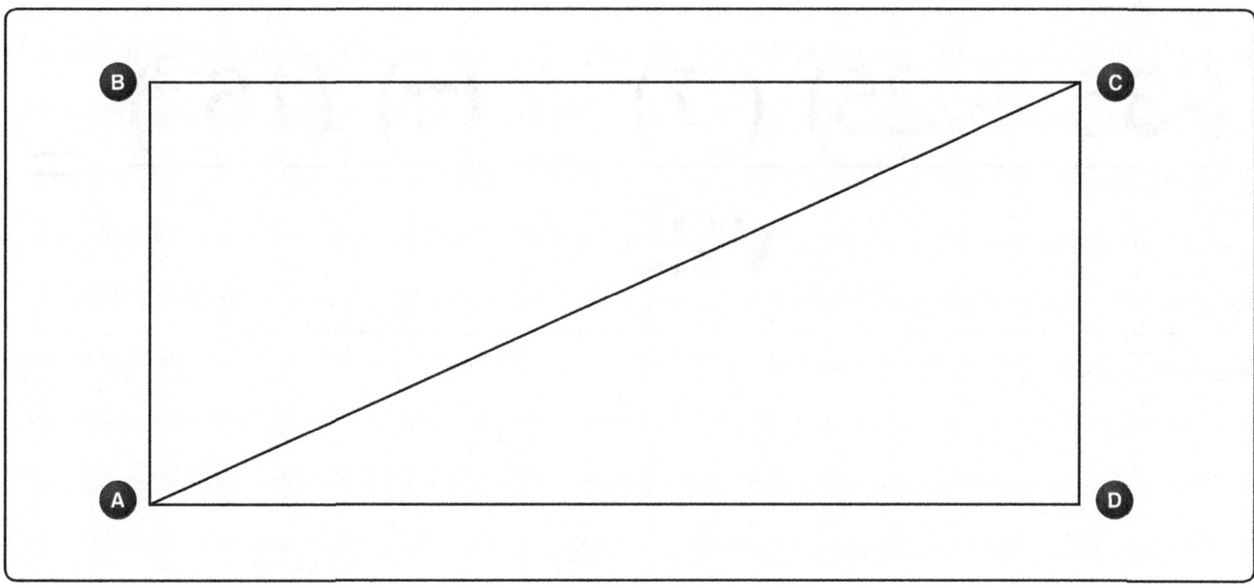

Figure 57. Triangle area.

Appendix 1

$$\frac{(-35 + 25)\ (-7) + (\pi)\ (16^{-2})}{\sqrt{25}} =$$

Figure 58. Equation.

$$\frac{-4\overline{)125}}{-6\overline{)-36}} =$$

Figure 59. Equation.

Appendix 1

$$\frac{(-5+23)(-2)+(3^{-3})(\sqrt{64})=}{-27\div 9}$$

Figure 60. Equation.

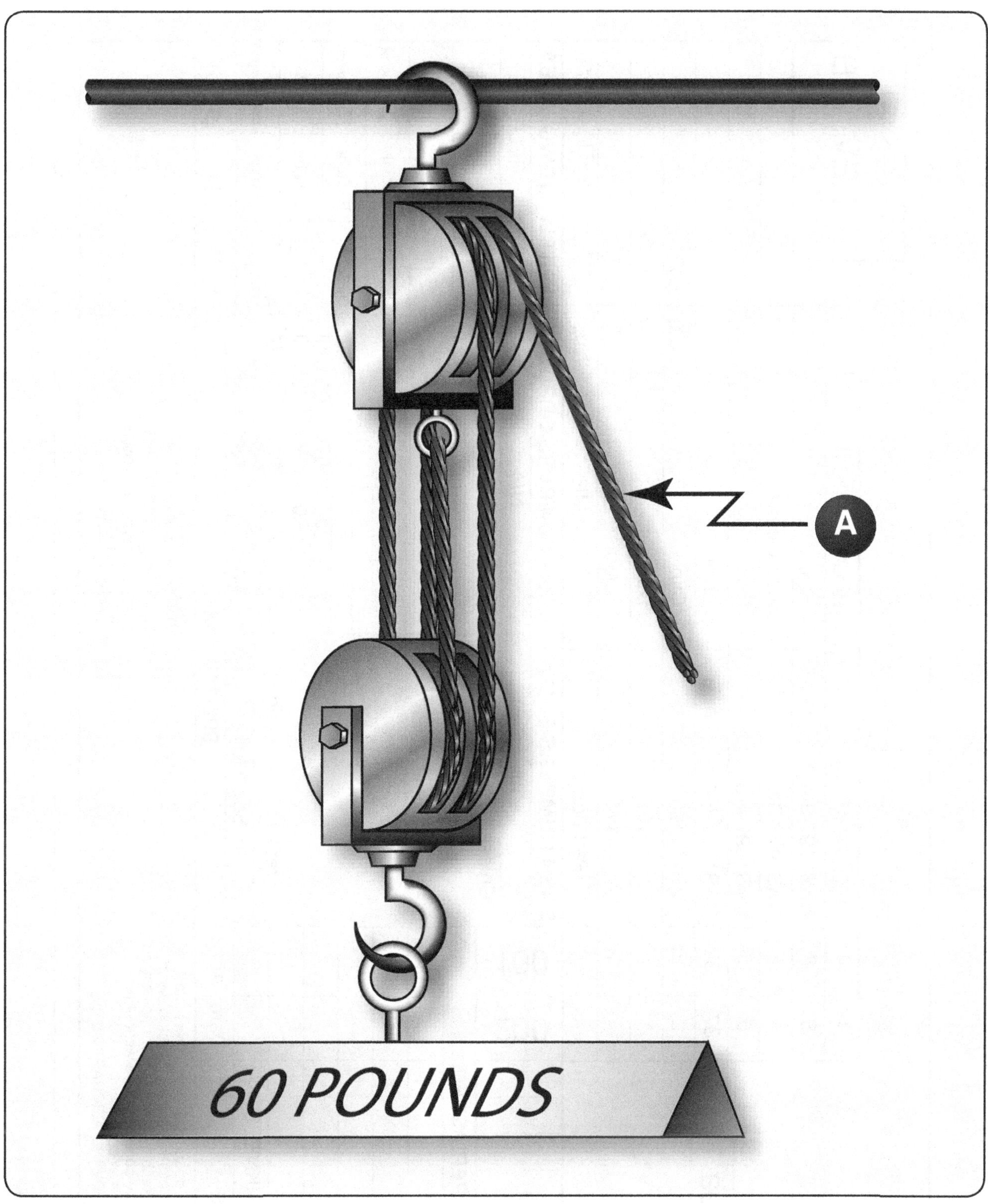

Figure 61. Physics.

REV. B

Area 1

-200	-100	Part number	NAME	stock size	MAT'L DESCR	MAT'L SPEC.	Zone
4	4	MS20470AD-4-4	Rivet				
8	8	NAS1097-3-4	Rivet				
4	4	NAS1473-3A	Domed Nutplate				
5	5	NAS1097-4-5	Rivet				
37	37	NAS1097-4-4	Rivet				
2	2	-103	Clip	.040 sheet	2024-T3 CLAD AL.		
1		-102	Doubler	.040 sheet	7075-0 AL.		
	1	-101	Doubler	.040 sheet	2024-T3 CLAD AL.		

REQ'd. PER ASSEM.

DASH NUMBERS SHOWN	DASH NUMBERS OPPOSITE	UNIT WT.	DWG. AREA
All	N/A	FIRST	RELEASE
Unless otherwise noted	For continuation see zone		

LET.	CHANGE	BY	Date	Appr.
B	ADD-200			
A	MAT'L THKNESS			

No. req. per Airplane		Type A/C	EFF
1	-200	36TCP	001-All
1	-200	36P	088-All
1	-200	36P	001-087

PROJECT	T. Smith	J. Smith
DESIGN	R. Eamer	R. Eamer
Engineer FAA D.E.R	G. Winn	G. Winn
DWG. Checker	I. Wright	I. Wright
DFTSMIN.	S. Linz	S. Linz

Break all sharp edges

Scale full

992-148-XXX

1 The use of this document shall be restricted to conveyance of information to customers of vendors only. Neither classified nor unclassified documents may be reproduced without the written consent of THE SPEEDWIND AIRCRAFT CORP.

Speedwind aircraft engineering section last chance airport anytown OK 73125-1234

TAH

Figure 62. Maintenance data - part 1 of 3.

AREA 2

GENERAL NOTES - 100

1. ALL BENDS +/– .5 deg.
2. All holes +/– .003.
3. Apply Alodine 1,000.
4. Prime with MIL-P-23377 or equivalent.
5. Trim S-1 C just aft of the clip at STA. 355.750 and forward of the front face of the STA. 370.25 frame and remove from the airplane.
6. Position the –101 doubler as shown. Install wet with NAS1097AD-4-4 and -4-5 rivets and a faying surface seal of PR 1,422. Pick up the rivet row that was in S-1 C and the aft rivets in sta. 370.25. Tie doubler into front frame with clips as shown using MS20470AD-4-4 rivets through the clips and the frame.
7. Install 4 NAS1473-3A nutplates with NAS1097-3-4 rivets through the skin and doubler to retain the antenna.
8. Strip paint and primer from under the antenna footprint.
9. Treat skin with Alodine 1,000.
10. Install antenna and apply weather seal fillet around antenna base.

AREA 3

GENERAL NOTES - 200

Note: P.S. = Process Specification
IAW = in accordance with

1. ALL BENDS IAW P.S. 1,000.
2. All holes IAW P.S. 1,015.
3. Heat treat –102 to –T6 IAW P.S. 5,602.
4. Alodine IAW P.S. 10,000.
5. Prime IAW P.S. 10,125.
6. Trim S-1 C just aft of the clip at STA. 355.750 and forward of the front face of the STA. 370.25 frame and remove from airplane.
7. Position the –102 doubler as shown. Install wet with NAS1097AD-4-4 and -4-5 rivets, and a faying surface seal IAW P.S. 41,255. Pick up the rivet row that was S-1 C and the aft rivets in STA. 370.25. Add two edge rows as shown. Tie doubler into front frame with clips as shown using MS20470AD-4-4 rivets through the clips and the frame.
8. Install 4 NAS1473-3A nutplates with NAS 1097-3-4 rivets through the skin and doubler to retain the antenna.
9. Strip paint and primer from under the antenna footprint.
10. Treat skin IAW P.S. 10,000.
11. Install antenna and apply weather seal fillet around antenna base.

Figure 62A. Maintenance data - part 2 of 3.

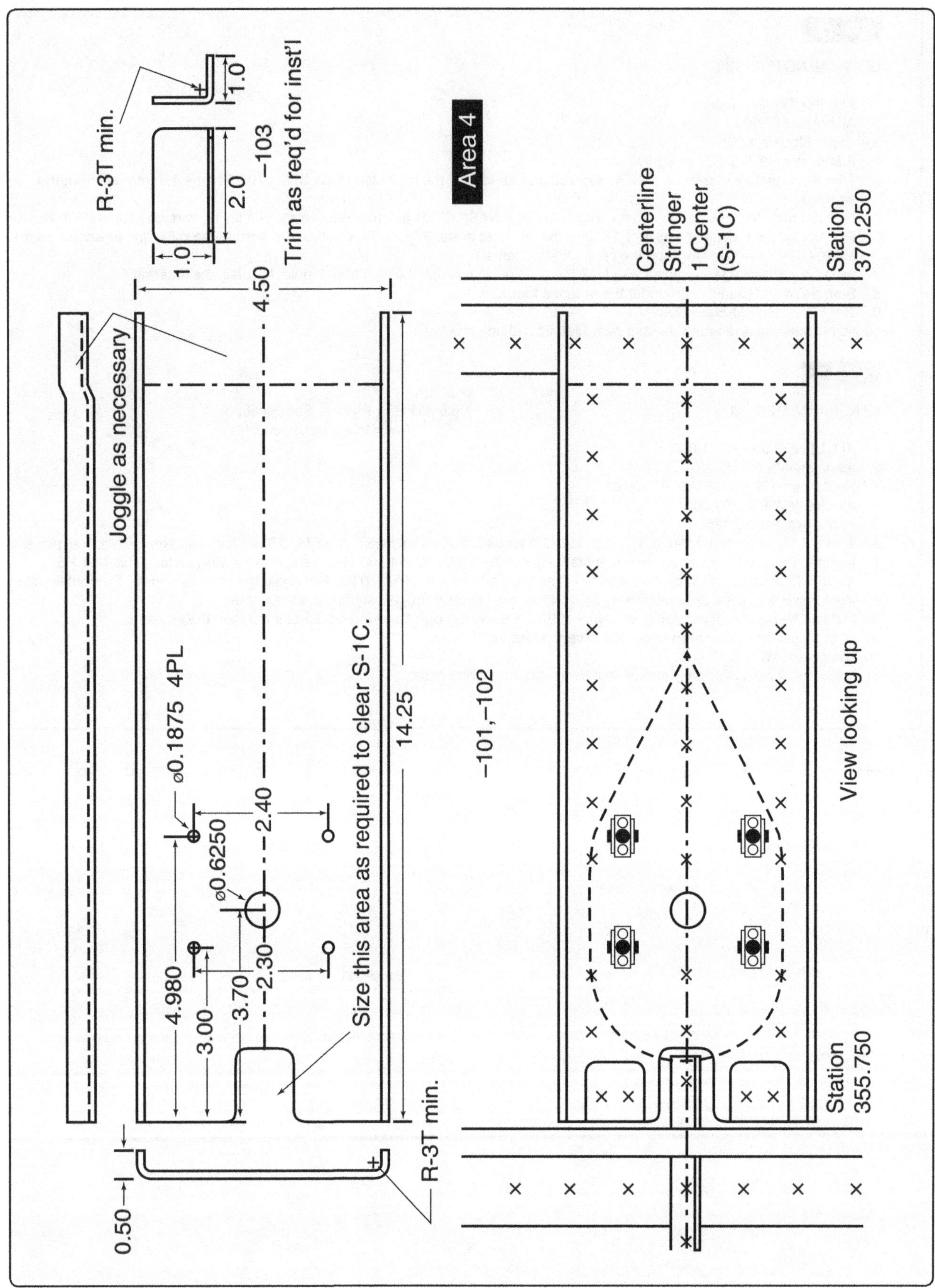

Figure 62B. Maintenance data - part 3 of 3.

The following is the compliance portion of an Airworthiness Directive.

"Compliance required as indicated, unless already accomplished:

I. Aircraft with less than 500 hours total time in service: Inspect in accordance with instructions below at 500 hours total time, or within the next 50 hours time in service after the effective date of this AD, and repeat after each subsequent 200 hours in service.

II. Aircraft with 500 hours through 1,000 hours total time in service: Inspect in accordance with instructions below within the next 50 hours time in service after the effective date of this AD, and repeat after each subsequent 200 hours in service.

III. Aircraft with more than 1,000 hours time in service: Inspect in accordance with instructions below within the next 25 hours time in service after the effective date of this AD, and repeat after each subsequent 200 hours in service."

Figure 63. Airworthiness directive excerpt.

Appendix 1

$$R_t = E^2/P$$

Figure 64. Resistance total.

1. $3.47 \times 10^4 = 34,700.$

2. $2(4^{10}) = 2,097,152.$

Figure 65. Scientific notation.

Appendix 1

$$-4 + 6 + 10^3 (\sqrt{1296}) =$$

Figure 66. Equation.

$$\frac{\sqrt{31} + \sqrt{43}}{(17)^2} =$$

Figure 67. Equation.

1. $(4.631)^5$
2. 4.631×10^5
3. 4.631×10^{-5}

Figure 68. Alternative answer.

$$(\sqrt{100} + \sqrt{36} - \sqrt{16}) =$$

Figure 69. Equation.

1. $(\sqrt{31}) + (\sqrt{43}) \div 17^2$
2. $(\sqrt{31}) + \sqrt{43}) \div 17^2$
3. $(\sqrt{31}) + (\sqrt{43}) - 17^2$

Figure 70. Alternative answer.

$$V = 1/6\pi D^3$$

Figure 71. Volume of a sphere.

APPENDIX 2

Aviation Mechanic Powerplant

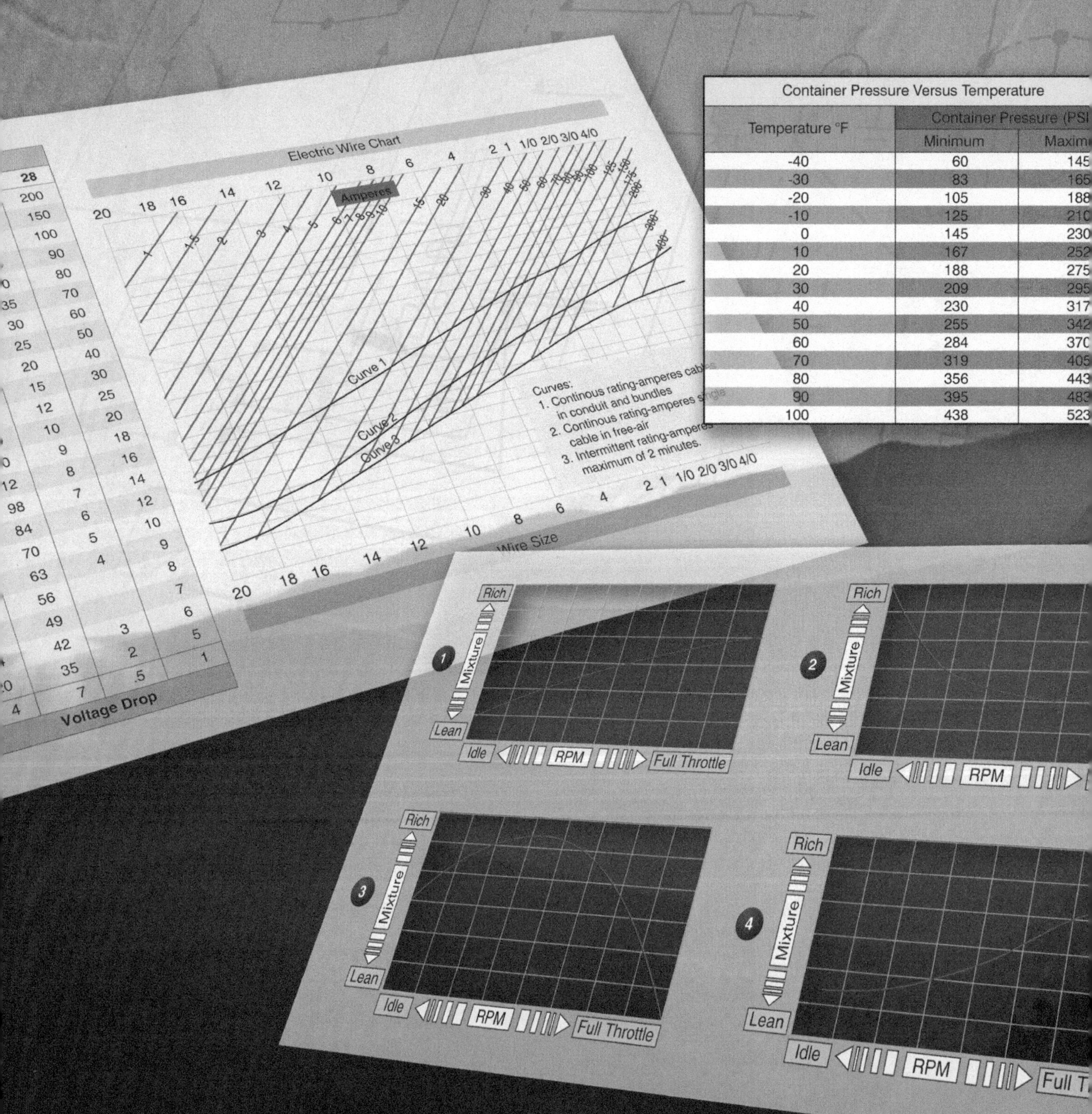

This is the compliance portion of an FAA Airworthiness Directive.

Compliance required as indicated:

(A) For model O-690 series engines, serial Nos. 101-40 through 5264-40 and IO-690 series engines, serial Nos. 101-48 through 423-48, compliance with (C) required within 25 hours' time in service after the effective date of this AD and every 100 hours' time in service thereafter.

(B) For model O-690 series engines, serial Nos. 5265-40 through 6129-40 and IO-690 series engines, serial Nos. 424-48 through 551-48, compliances with (C) required as follows.

(1) Within 25 hours' time in service after the effective date of this AD and every 100 hours' time in service thereafter for engines with more than 275 hours' time in service on the effective date of this AD.

(2) Prior to the accumulation of 300 hours total time in service and every 100 hours' time in service thereafter for engines with 275 hours or less time in service on the effective date of this AD.

(C) Inspect the oil pump drive shaft (P/N 67512) on applicable engines in accordance with instructions contained in Connin Service Bulletin No. 295. Any shafts which are found to be damaged shall be replaced before further flight. These inspections shall be continued until Connin P/N 67512 (redesigned) or P/N 74641 oil pump drive shaft is installed at which time the inspections may be discontinued.

Figure 1. Airworthiness directive excerpt.

Appendix 2

Container Pressure Versus Temperature		
Temperature °F	Container Pressure (PSIG)	
	Minimum	Maximum
-40	60	145
-30	83	165
-20	105	188
-10	125	210
0	145	230
10	167	252
20	188	275
30	209	295
40	230	317
50	255	342
60	284	370
70	319	405
80	356	443
90	395	483
100	438	523

Figure 2. Fire extinguisher pressure chart.

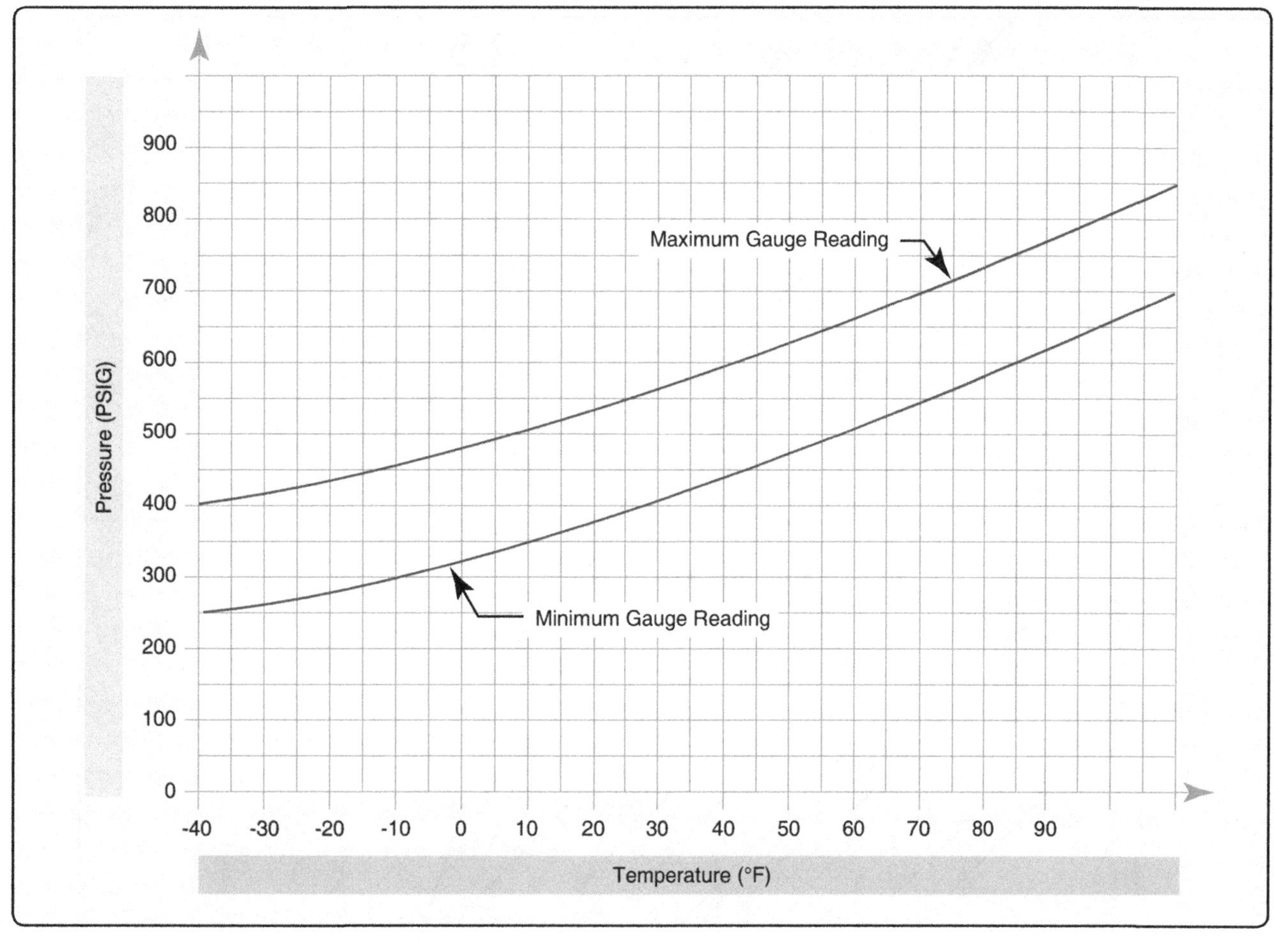

Figure 3. Fire extinguisher pressure chart.

Appendix 2

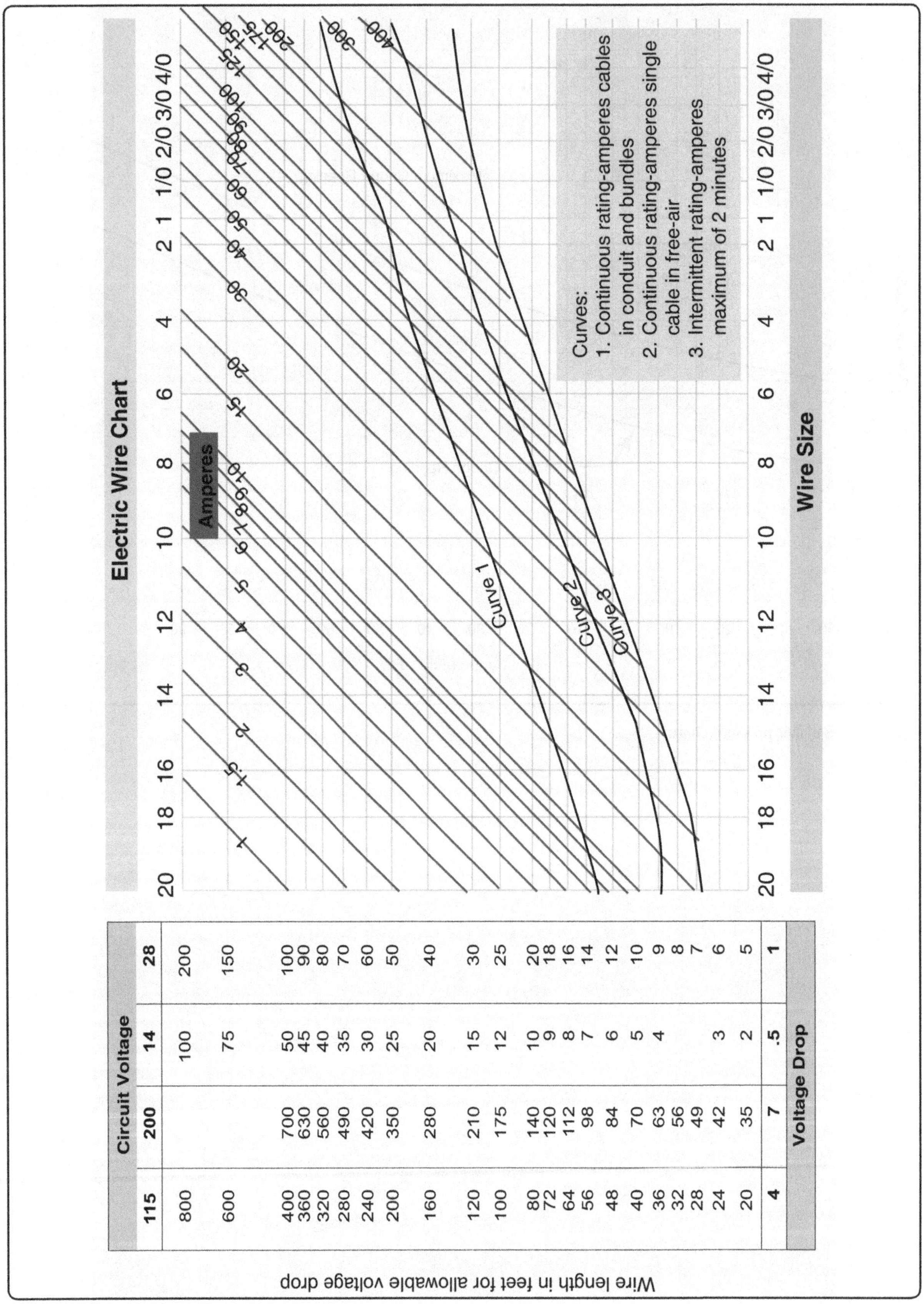

Electric Wire Chart

Circuit Voltage			
115	**200**	**14**	**28**
800		100	200
600		75	150
400	700	50	100
360	630	45	90
320	560	40	80
280	490	35	70
240	420	30	60
200	350	25	50
160	280	20	40
120	210	15	30
100	175	12	25
80	140	10	20
72	120	9	18
64	112	8	16
56	98	7	14
48	84	6	12
40	70	5	10
36	63	4	9
32	56		8
28	49		7
24	42	3	6
20	35	2	5
4	**7**	**.5**	**1**
Voltage Drop			

Wire length in feet for allowable voltage drop

Wire Size: 20 18 16 14 12 10 8 6 4 2 1 1/0 2/0 3/0 4/0

Amperes: 1 1.5 2 3 4 5 6 7 8 9 10 15 20 30 40 50 60 70 80 90 100 125 150 175 200 300 400

Curve 1
Curve 2
Curve 3

Curves:
1. Continuous rating-amperes cables in conduit and bundles
2. Continuous rating-amperes single cable in free-air
3. Intermittent rating-amperes maximum of 2 minutes

Figure 4. Electric wire chart.

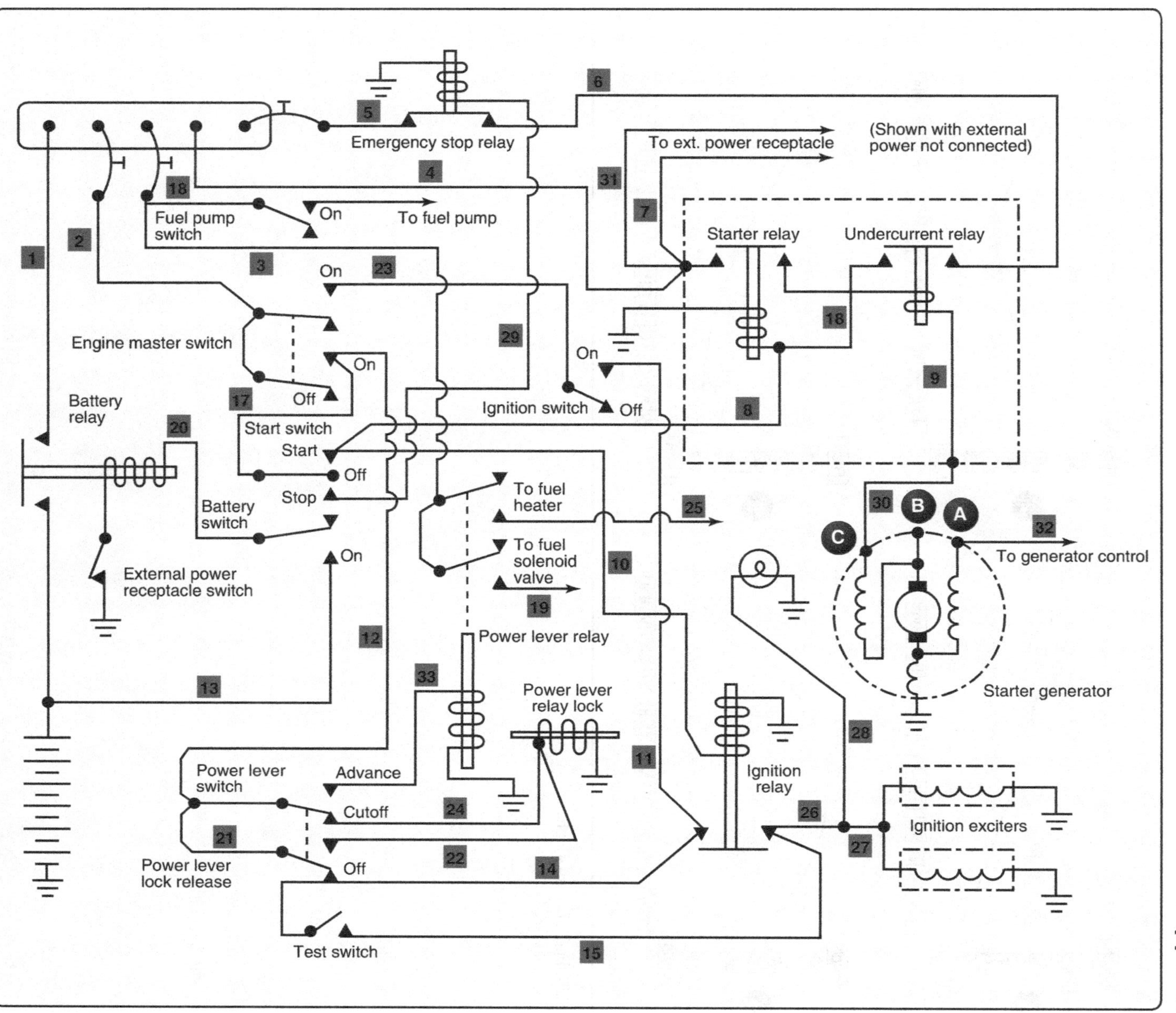

Figure 5. Starter-generator circuit.

Appendix 2

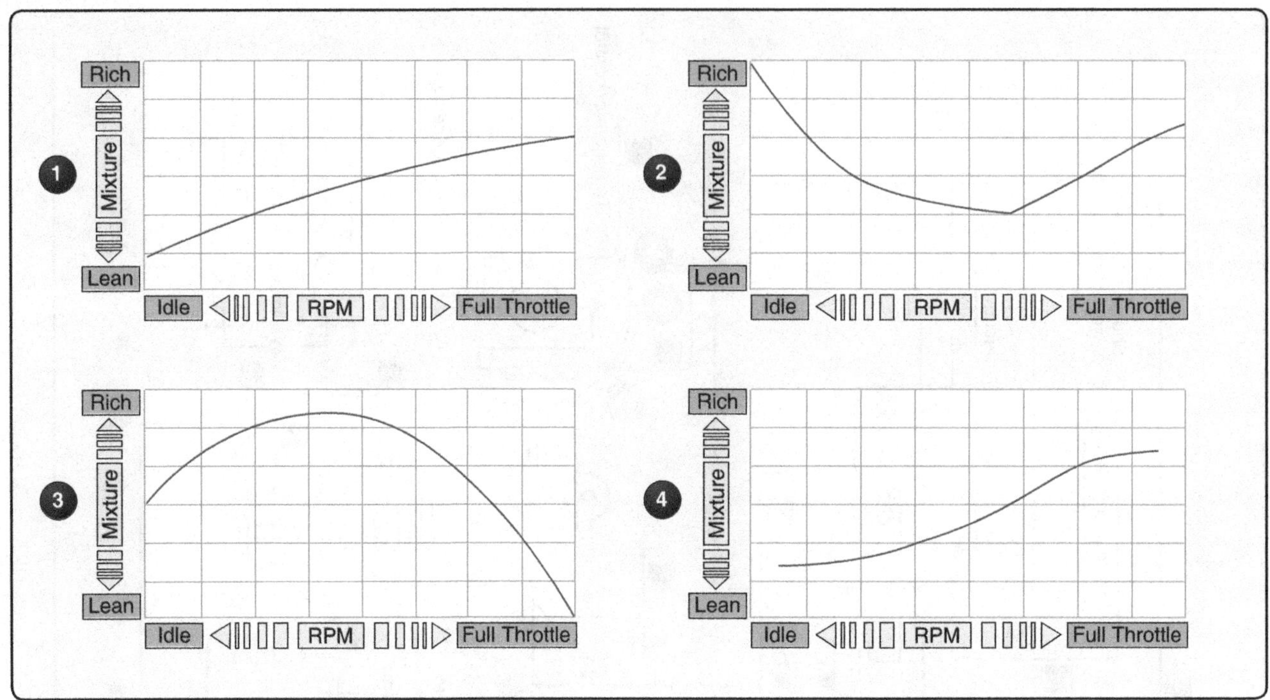

Figure 6. Fuel/air ratio graphs.

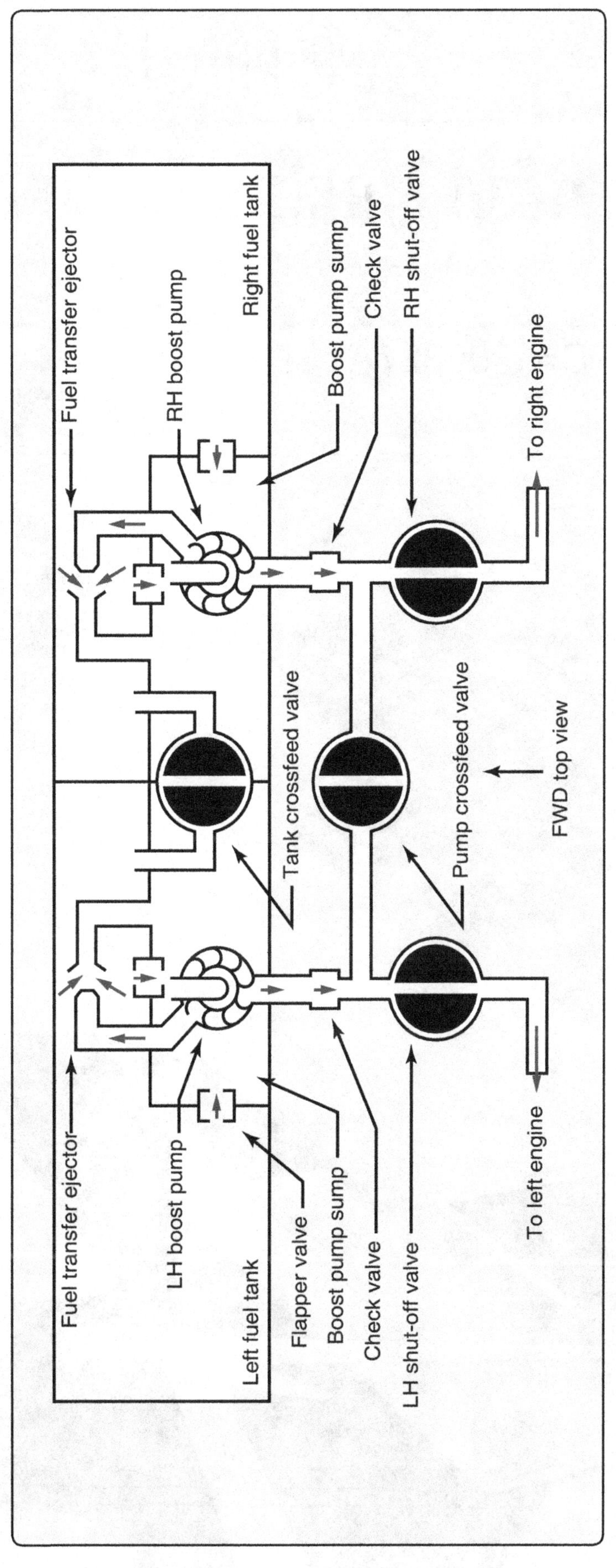

Figure 7. Fuel system.

APPENDIX 3

Aviation Mechanic Airframe

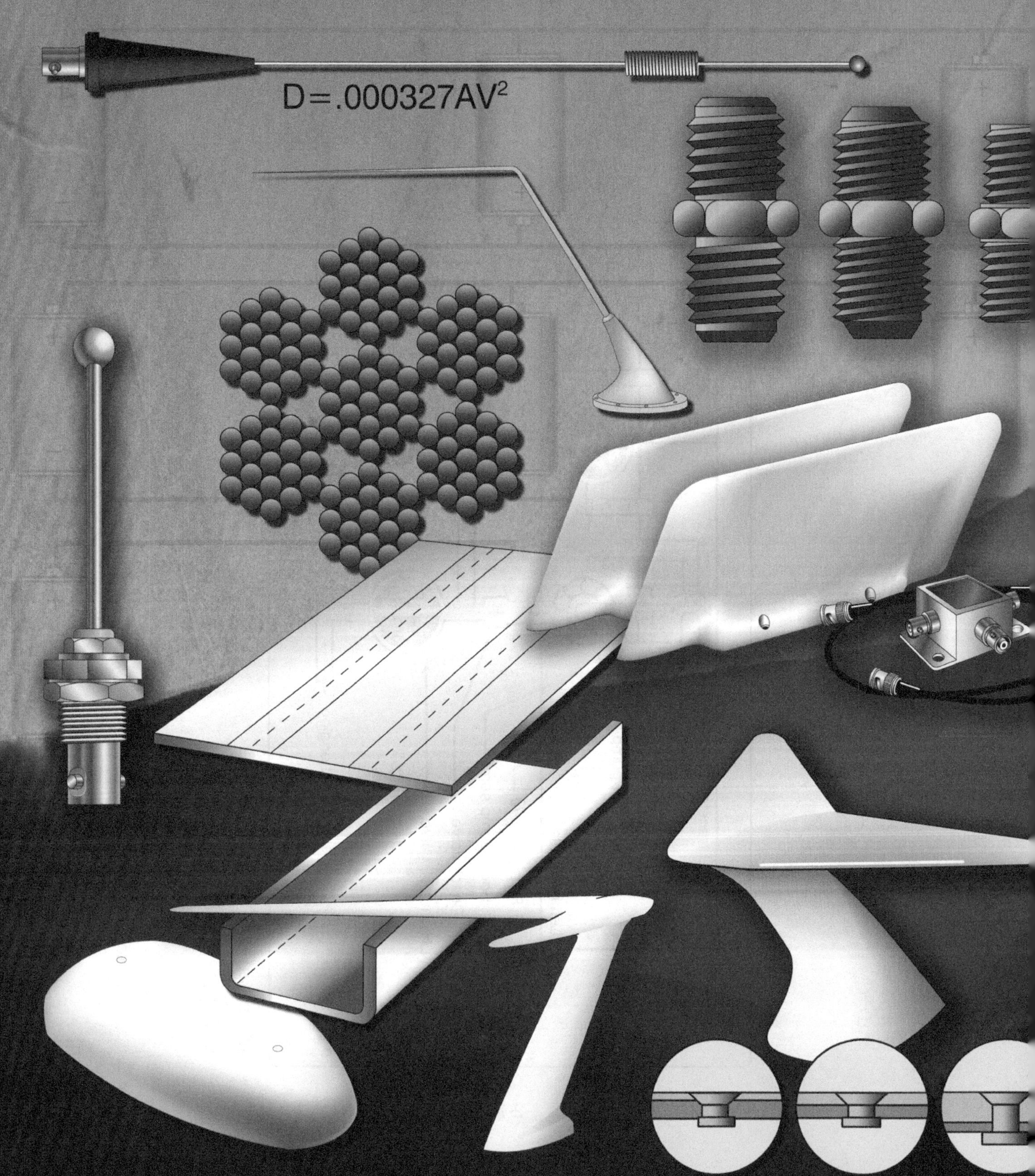

Appendix 3

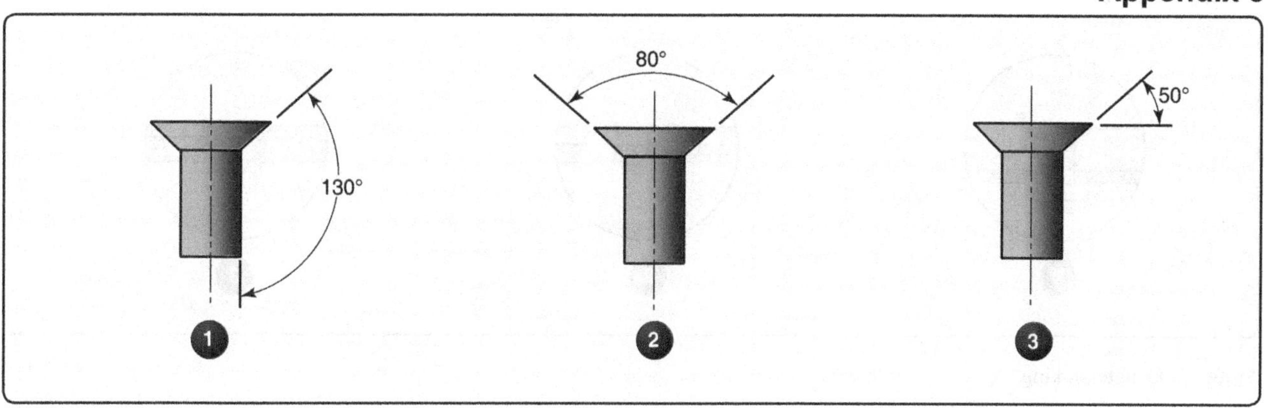

Figure 1. Rivets.

Appendix 3

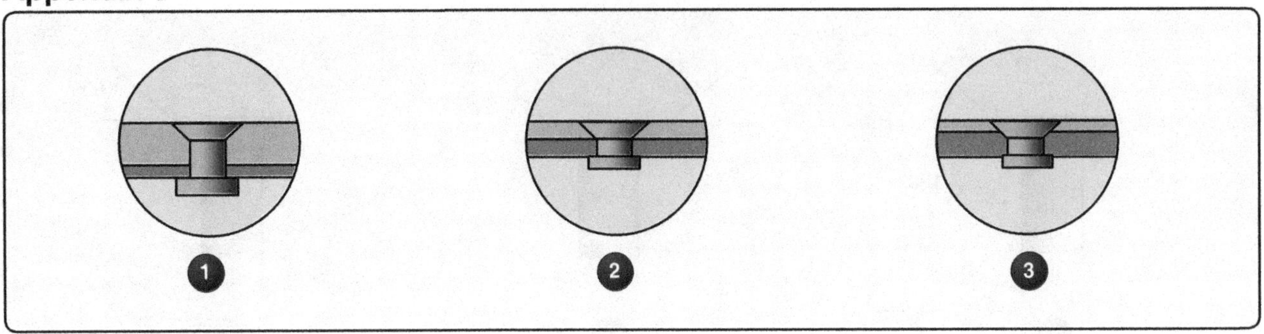

Figure 2. Countersinking.

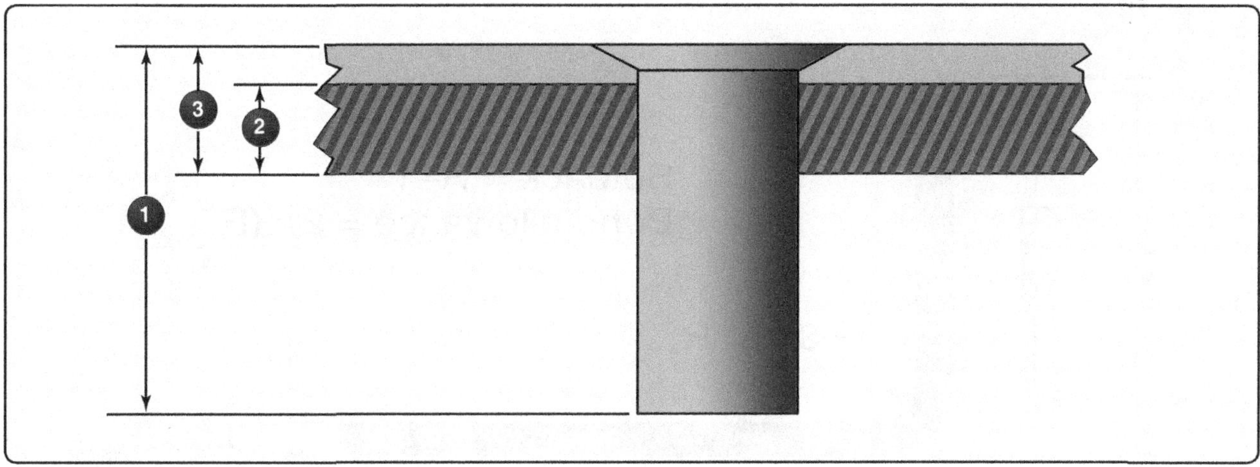

Figure 3. Grip length.

Appendix 3

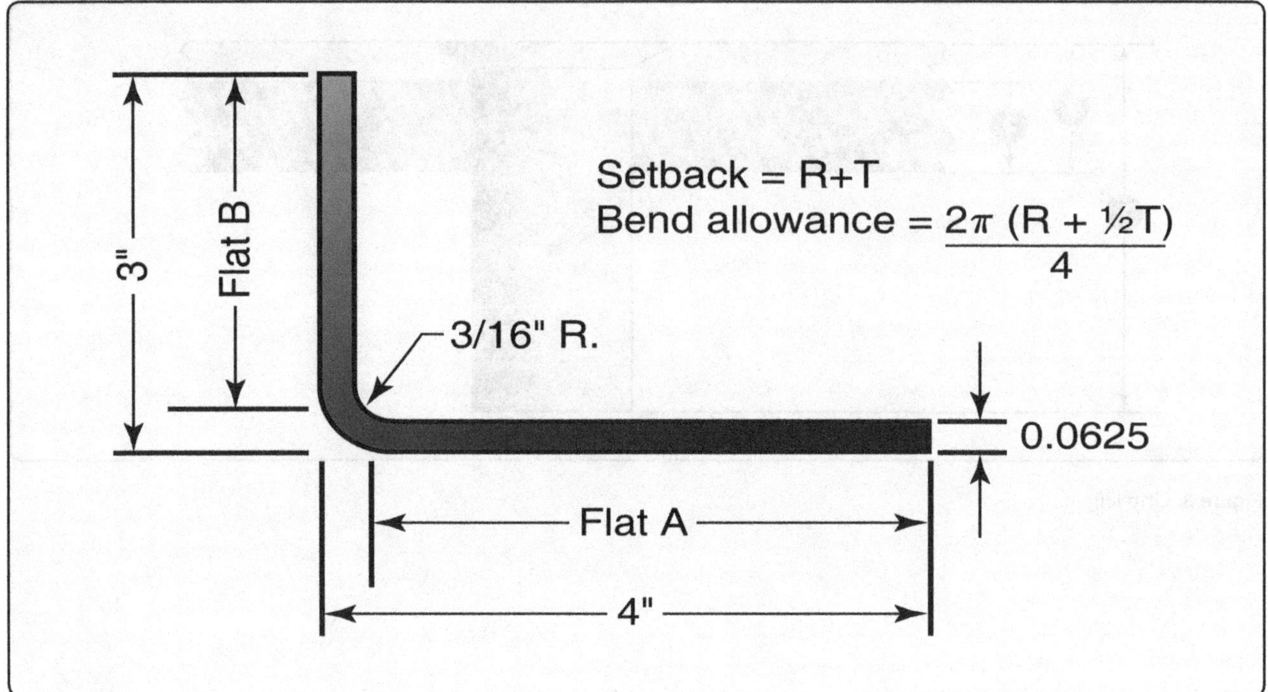

Figure 4. Bending sheet metal.

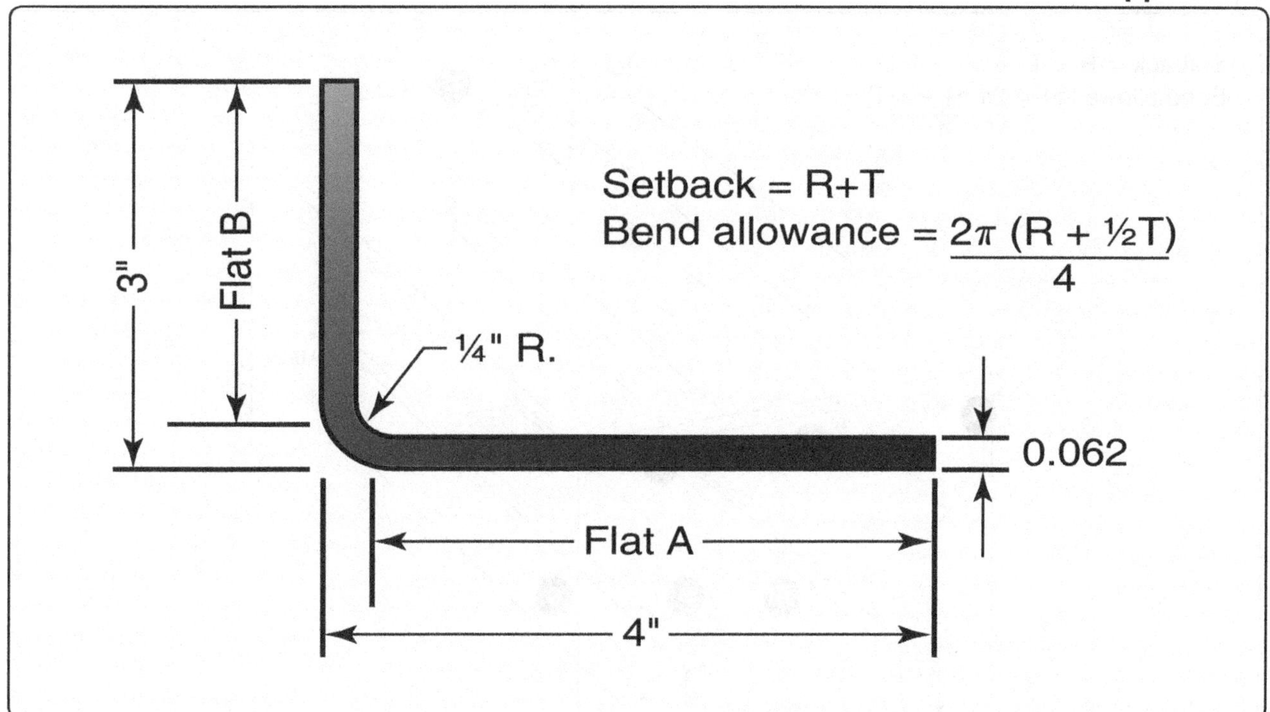

Figure 5. Sheet metal layout.

Appendix 3

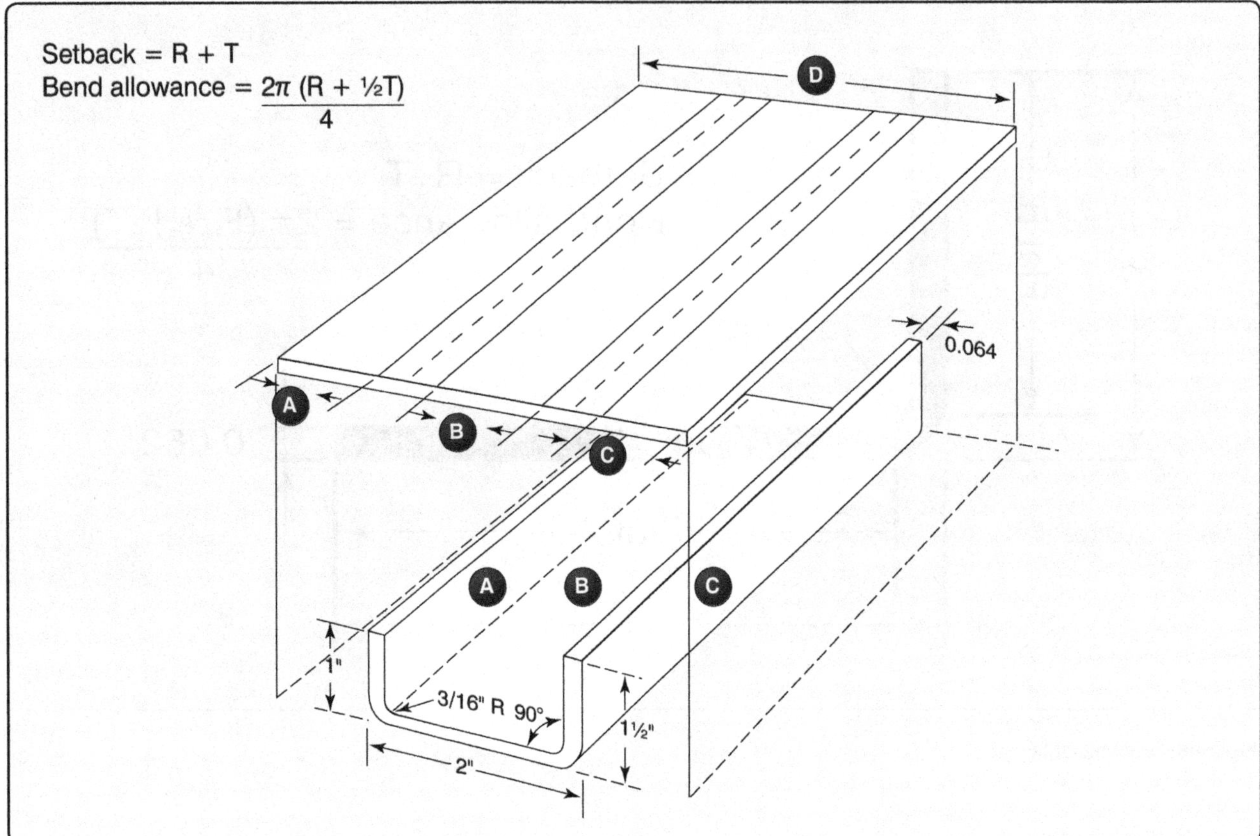

Figure 6. Sheet metal layout.

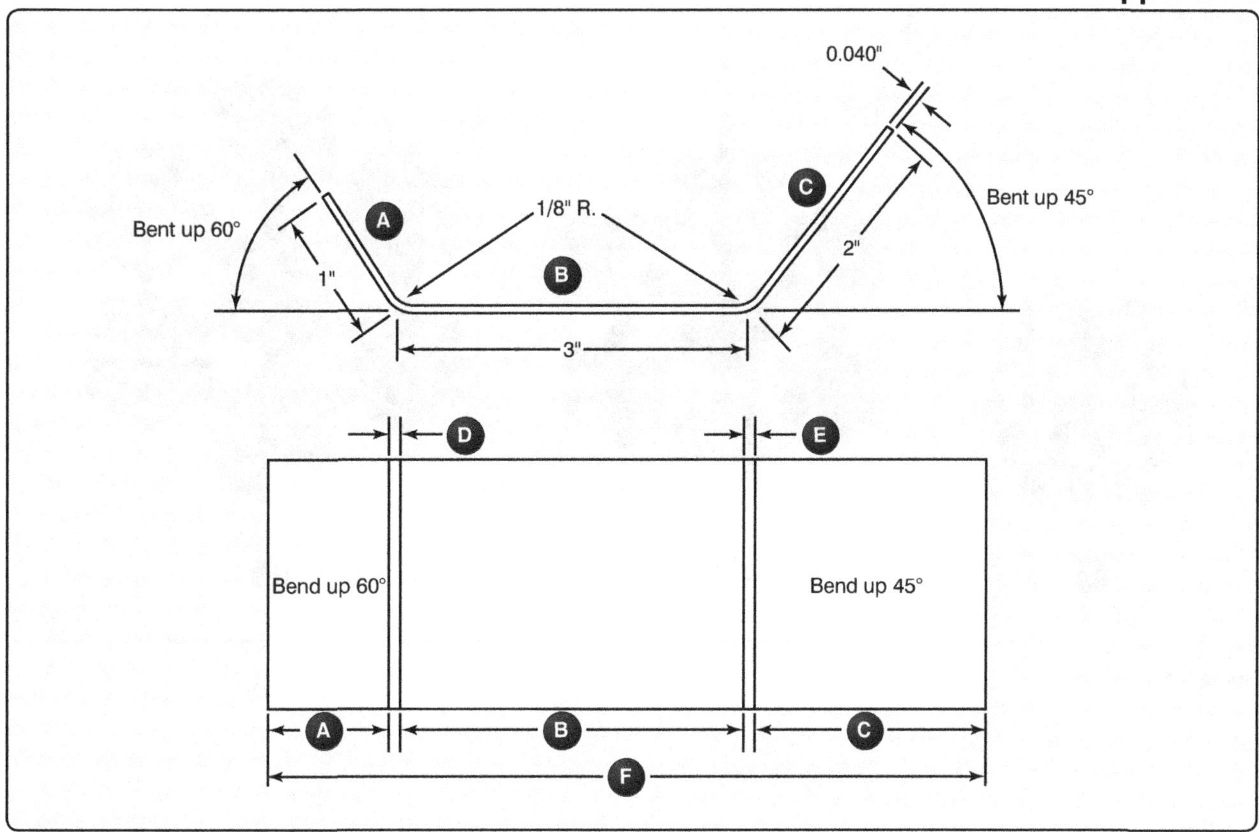

Figure 7. Sheet metal layout.

Appendix 3

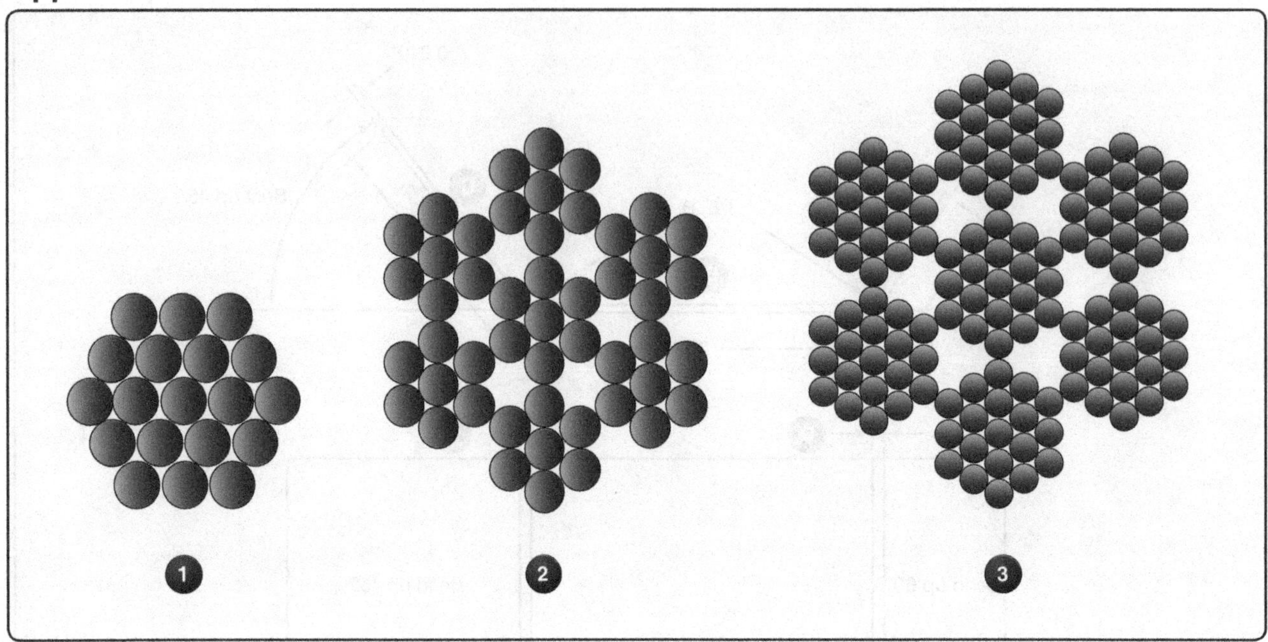

Figure 8. Control cable.

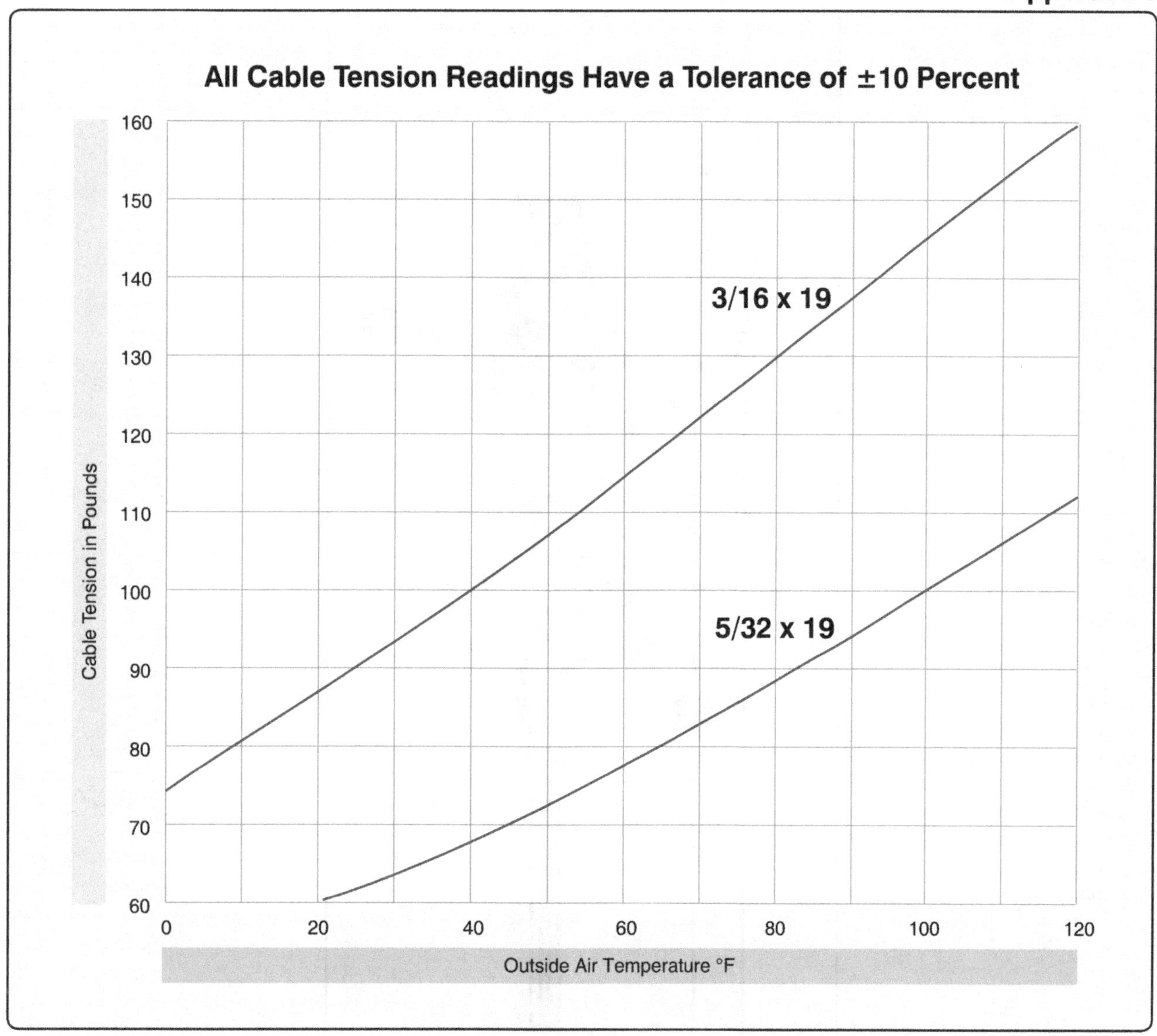

Figure 9. Cable tension chart.

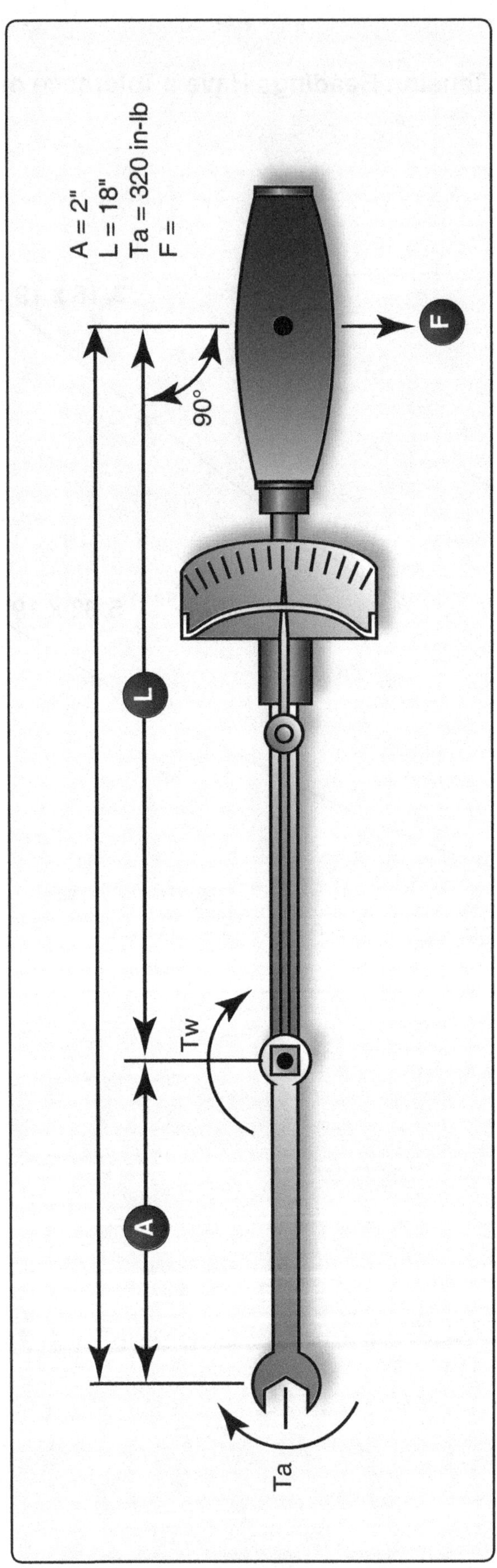

Figure 10. Torque value.

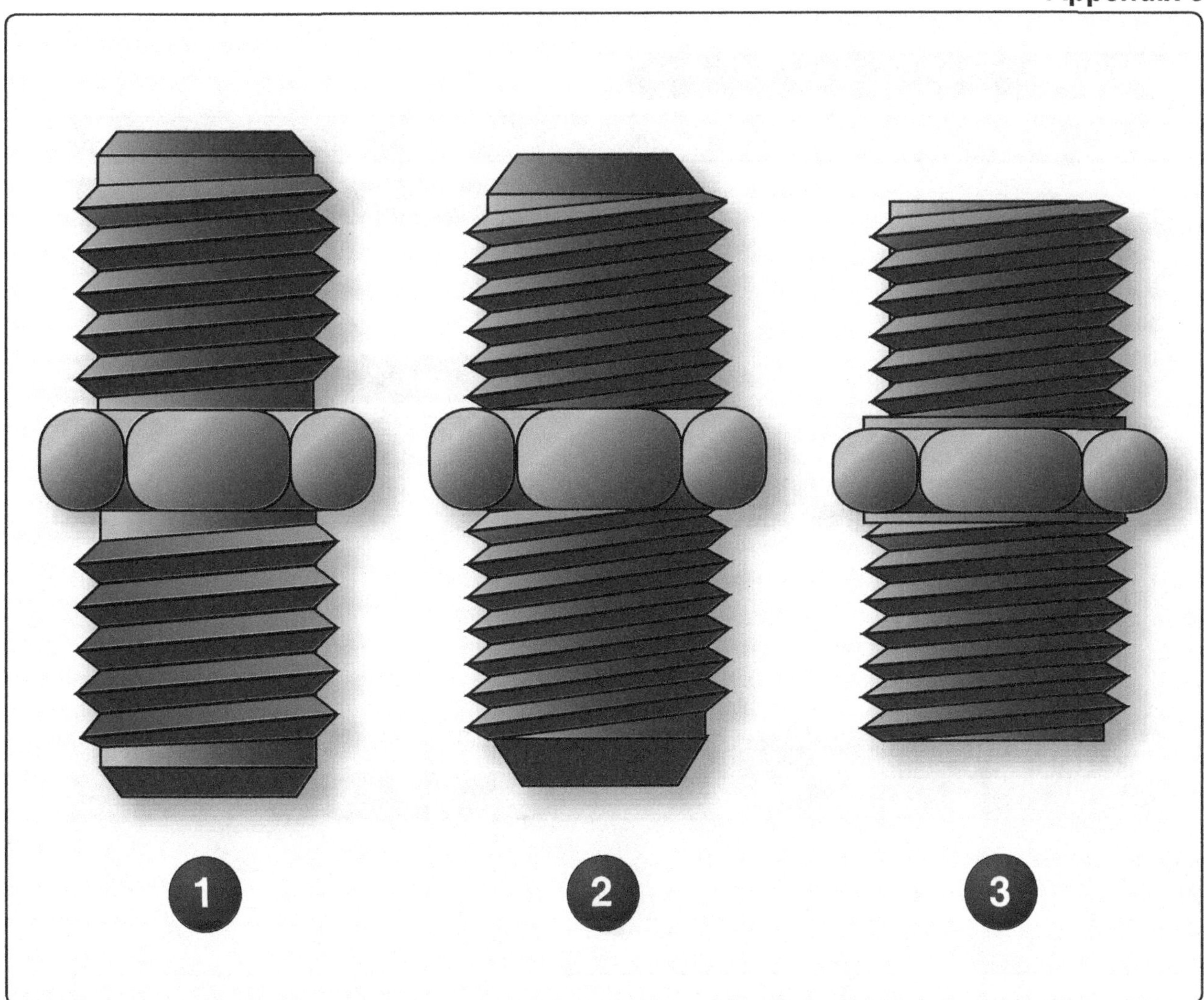

Figure 11. Fittings.

Appendix 3

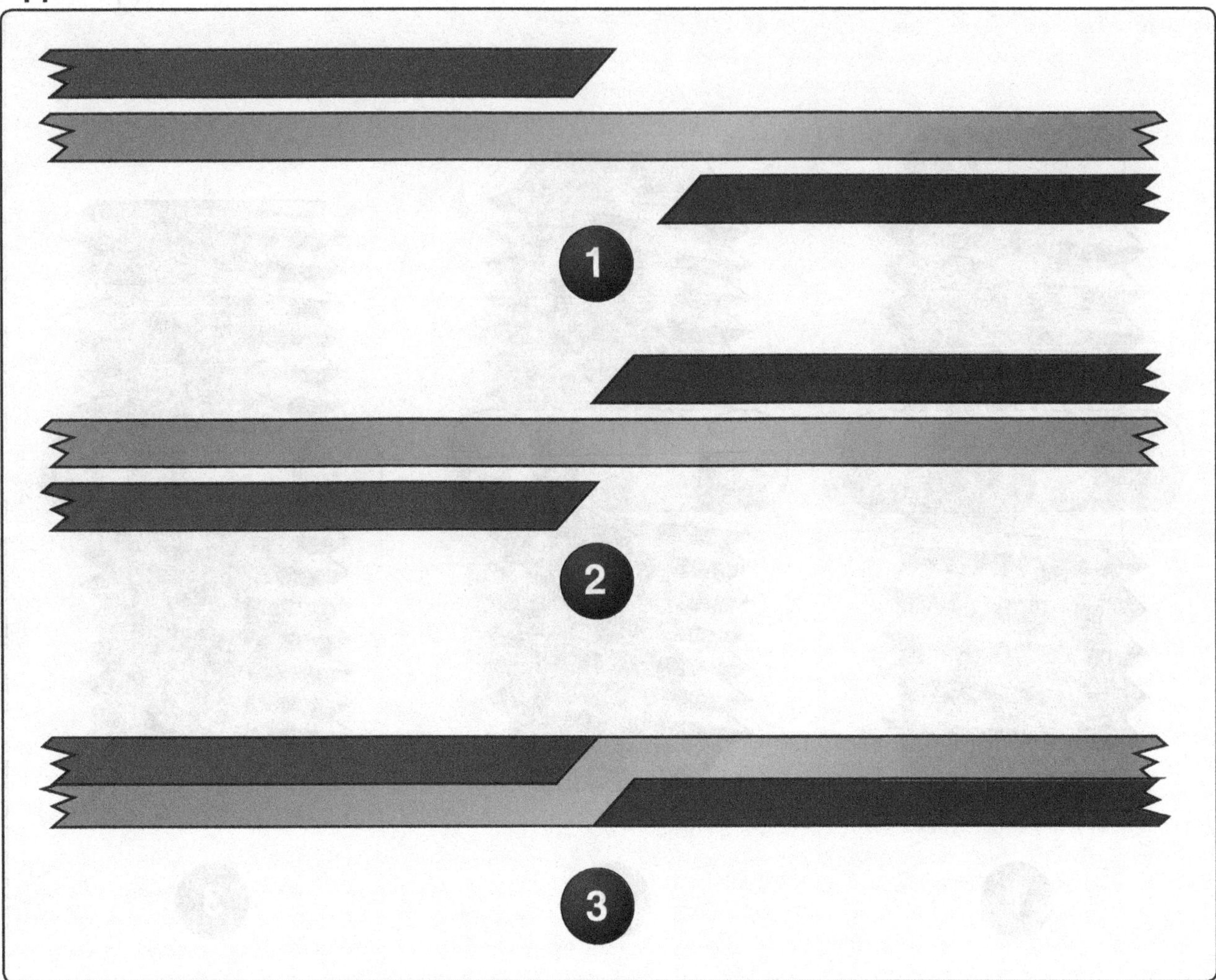

Figure 12. Backup rings.

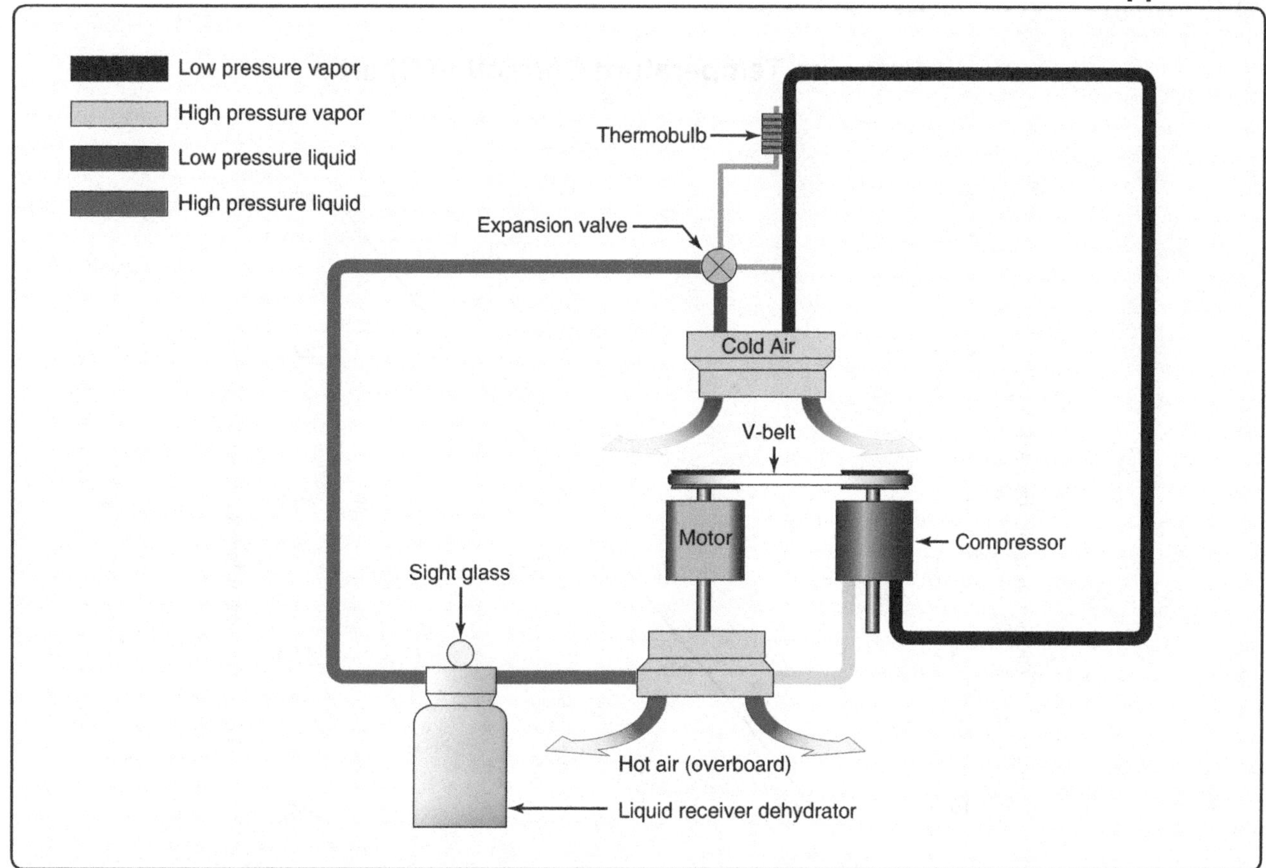

Figure 13. Cooling system.

Appendix 3

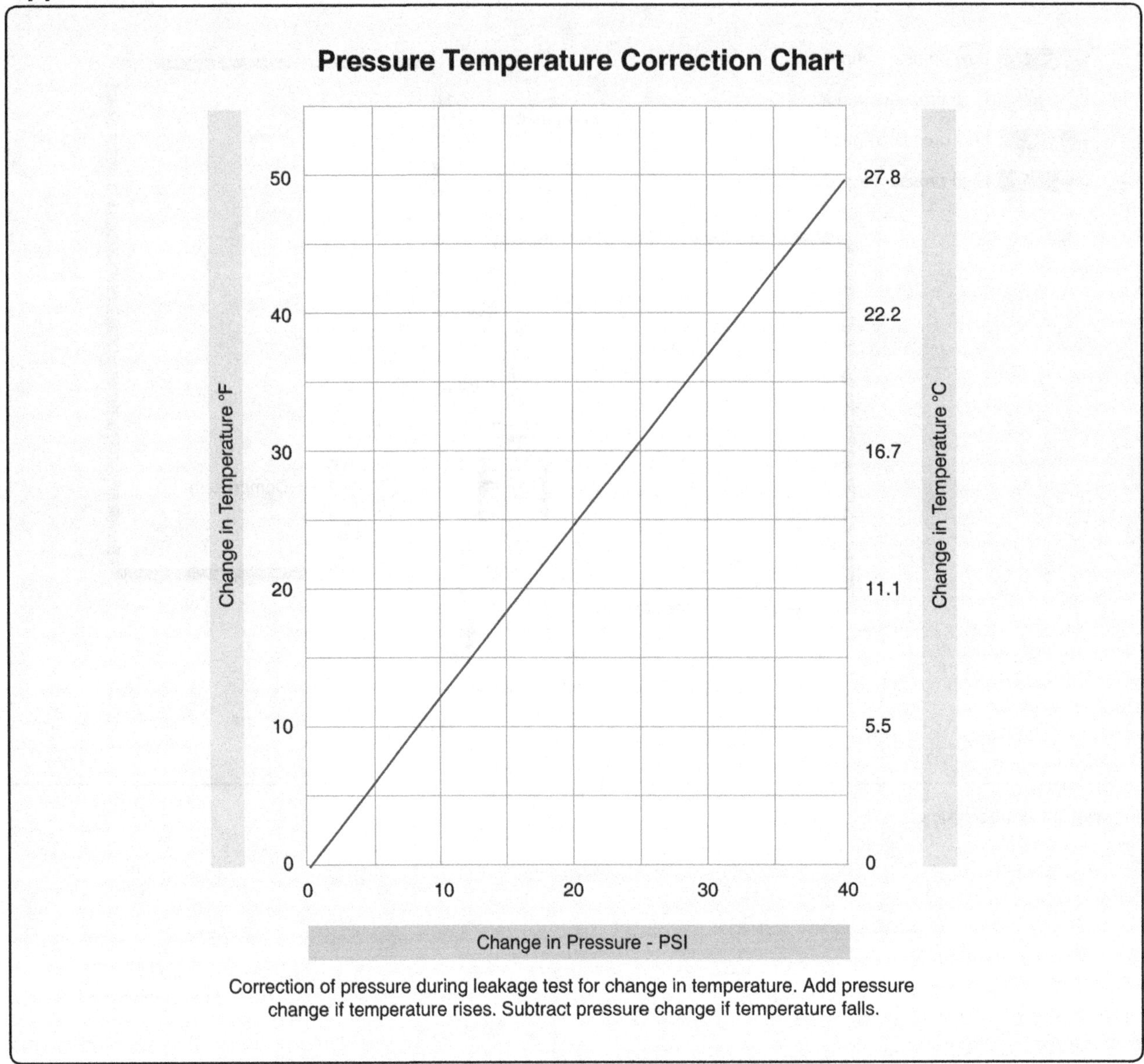

Figure 14. Pressure temperature correction chart.

$$D = .000327AV^2$$

Figure 15. Formula.

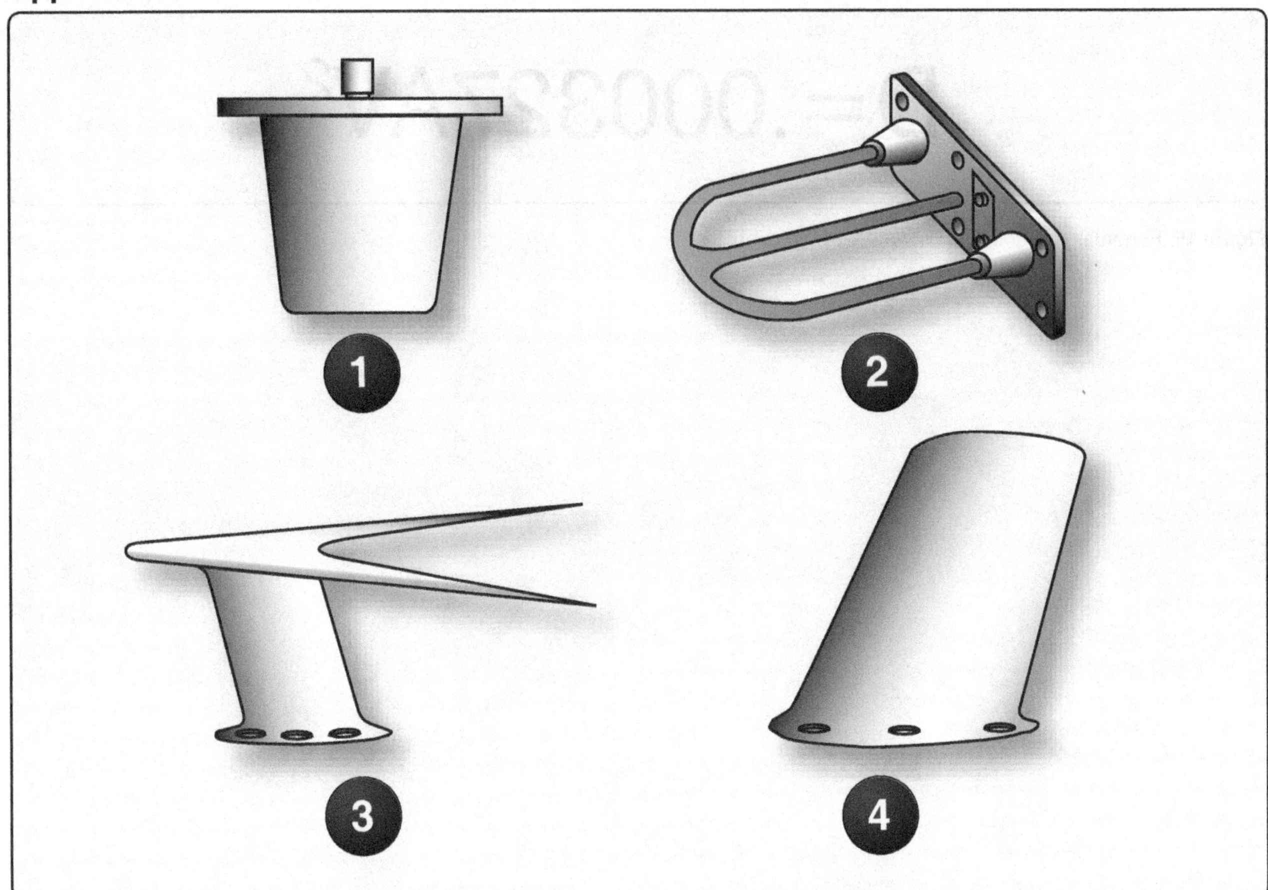

Figure 16. Antennas.

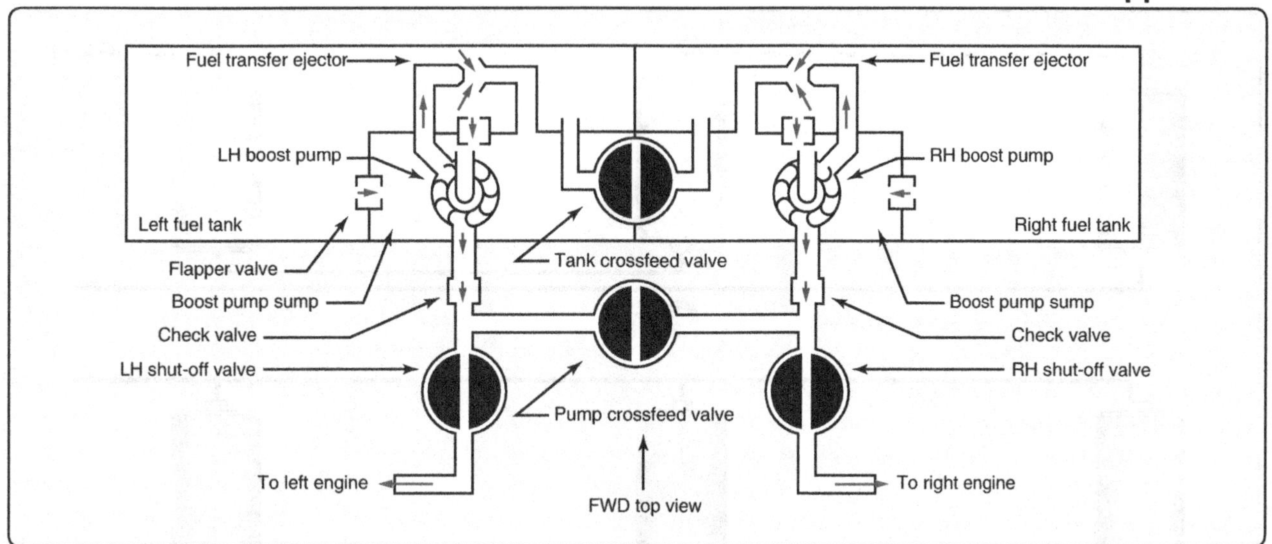

Figure 17. Fuel system.

Appendix 3

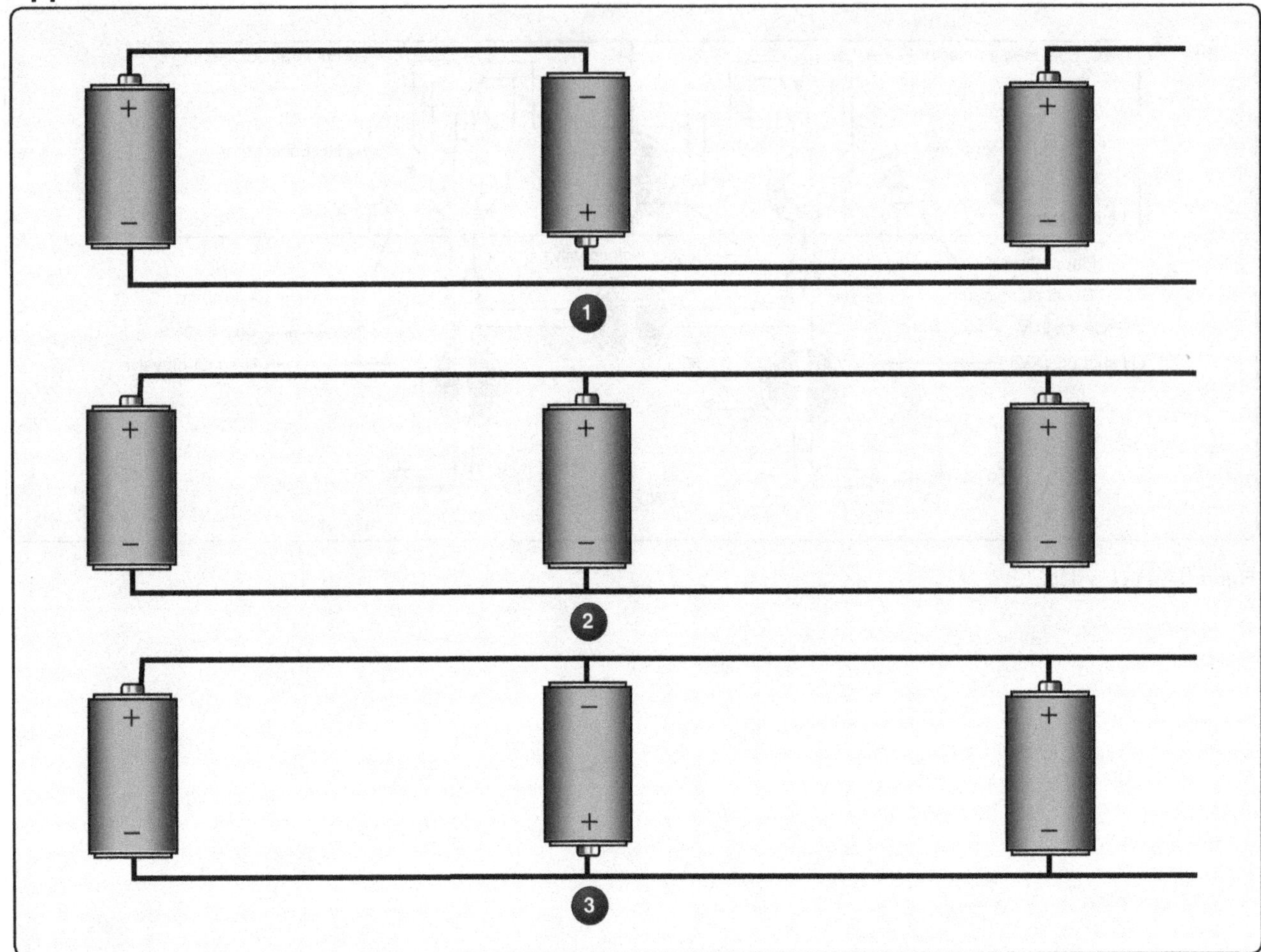

Figure 18. Battery connections.

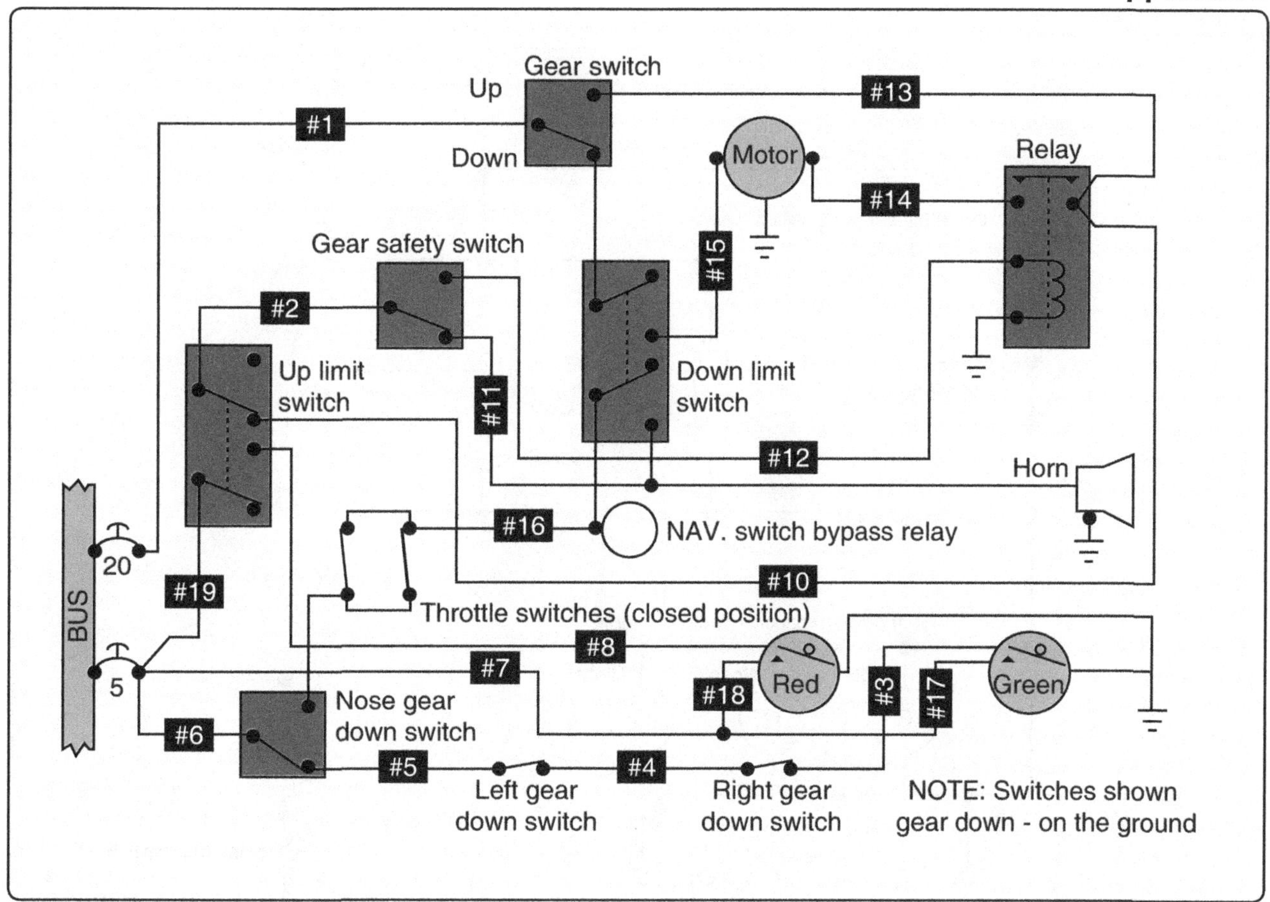

Figure 19. Landing gear circuit.

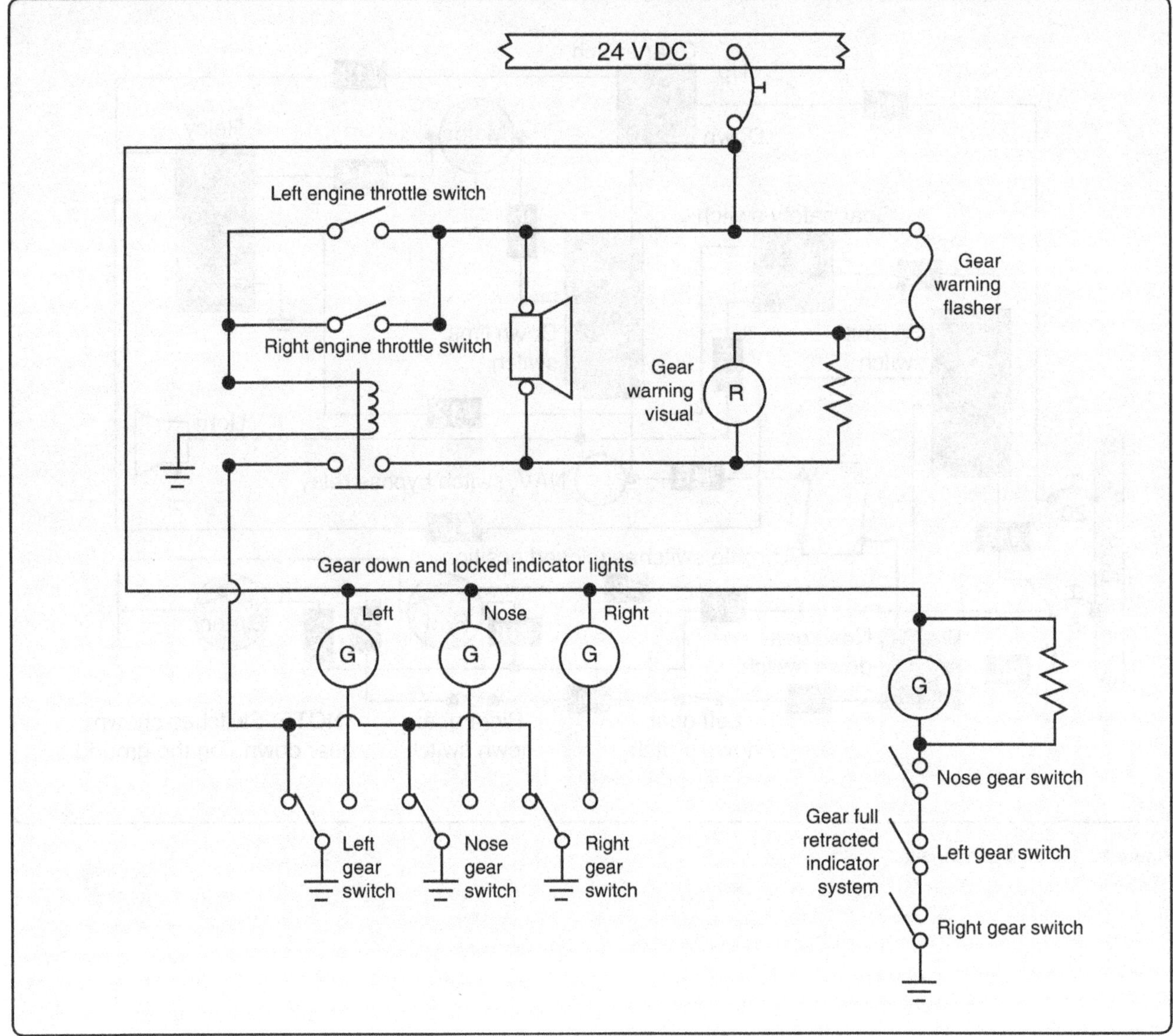

Figure 20. Landing gear circuit.

Container Pressure Versus Temperature		
Temperature °F	Container Pressure (PSIG)	
	Minimum	Maximum
-40	60	145
-30	83	165
-20	105	188
-10	125	210
0	145	230
10	167	252
20	188	275
30	209	295
40	230	317
50	255	342
60	284	370
70	319	405
80	356	443
90	395	483
100	438	523

Figure 21. Fire extinguisher chart.

Appendix 3

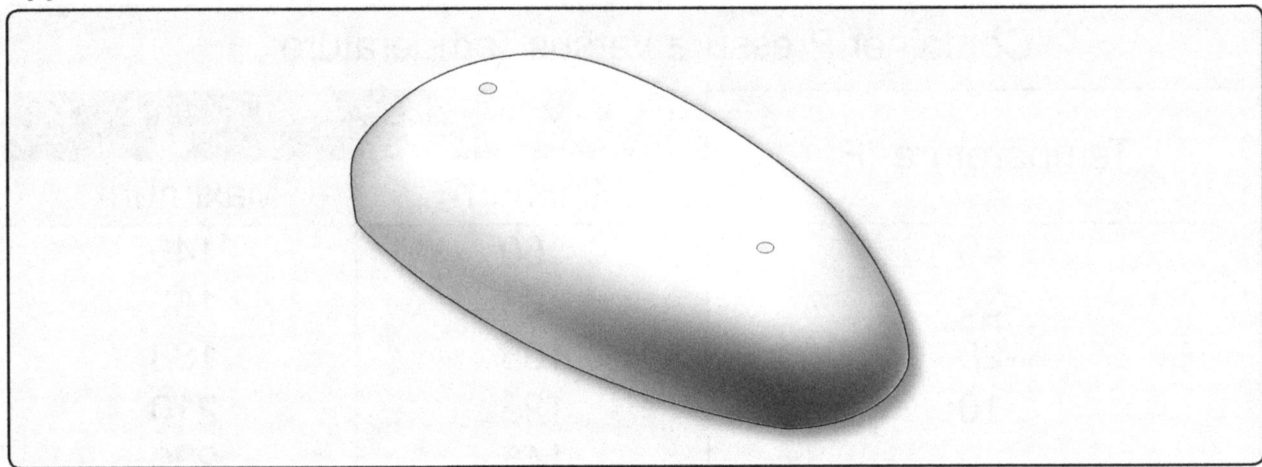

Figure 22. Antenna.

Figure 23. Antenna.

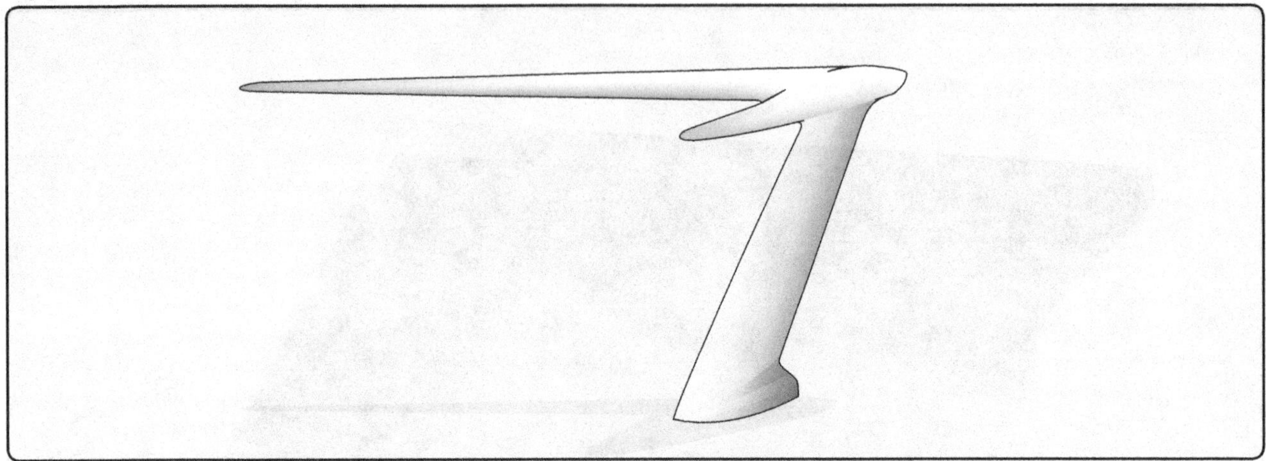

Figure 24. Antenna.

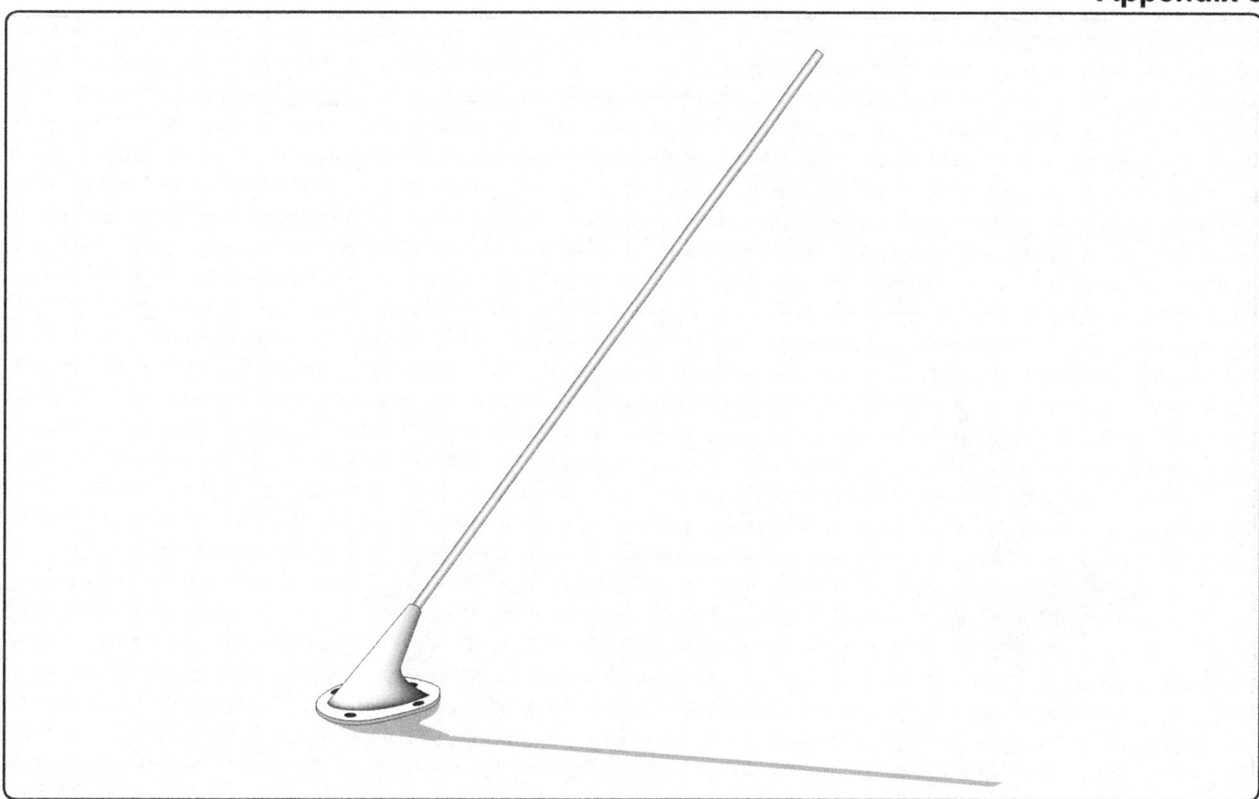

Figure 25. Antenna.

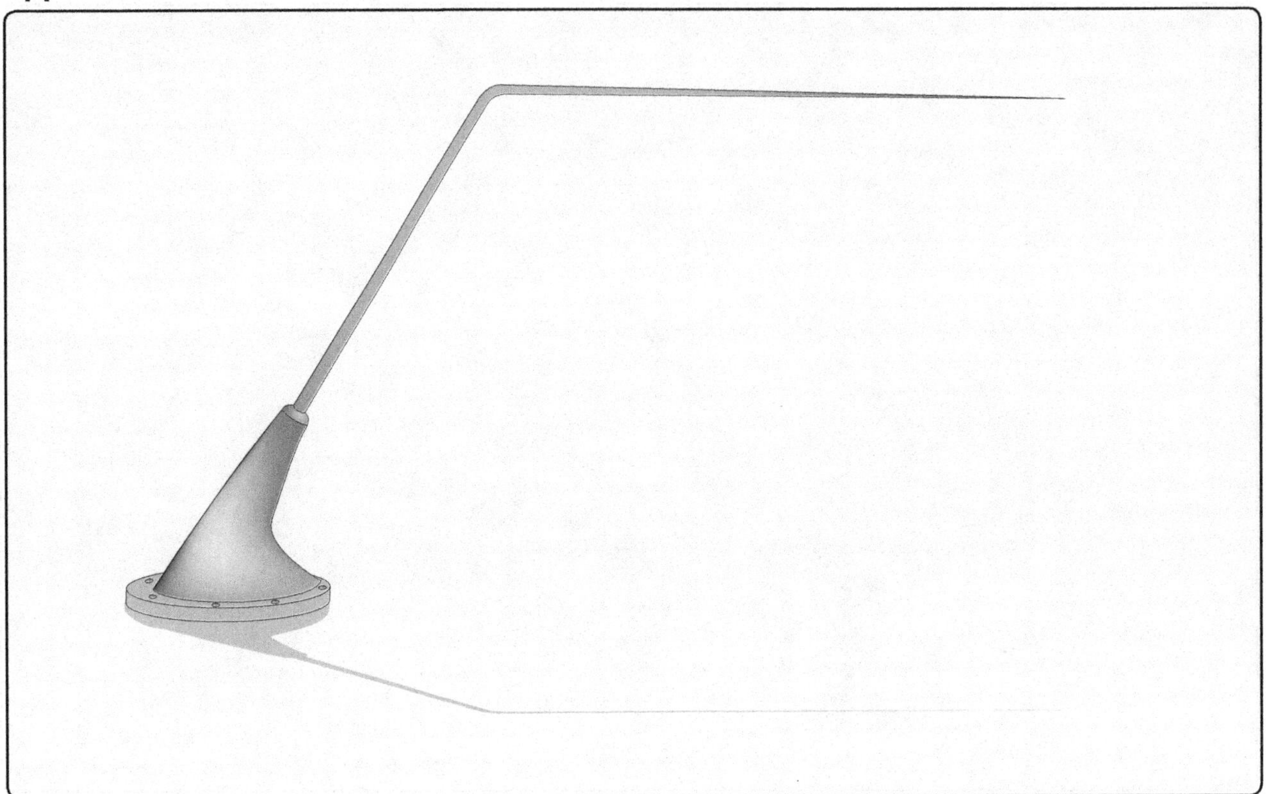

Figure 26. Antenna.

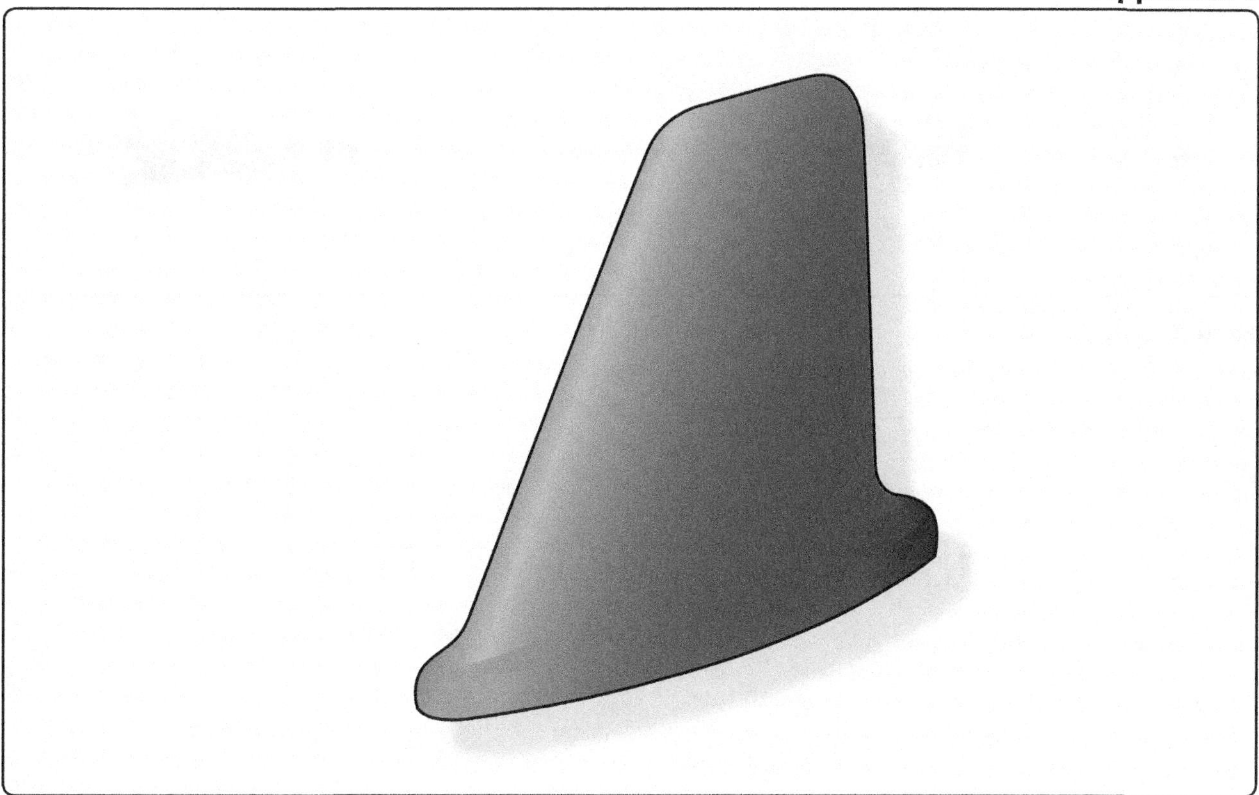

Figure 27. Antenna.

Appendix 3

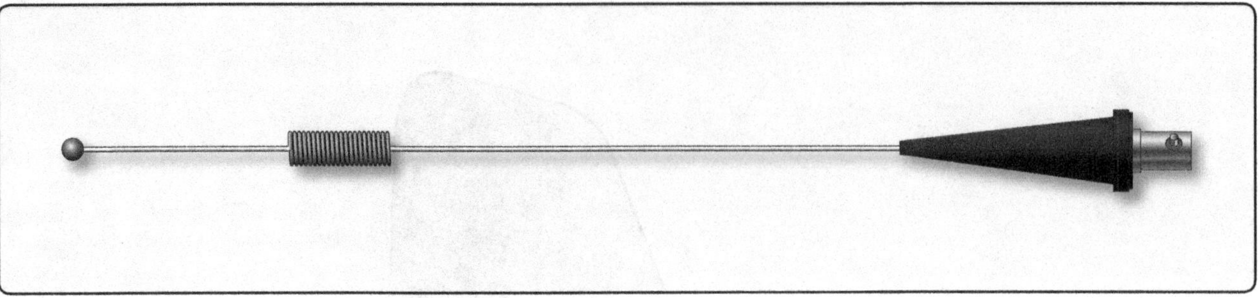

Figure 28. Antenna.

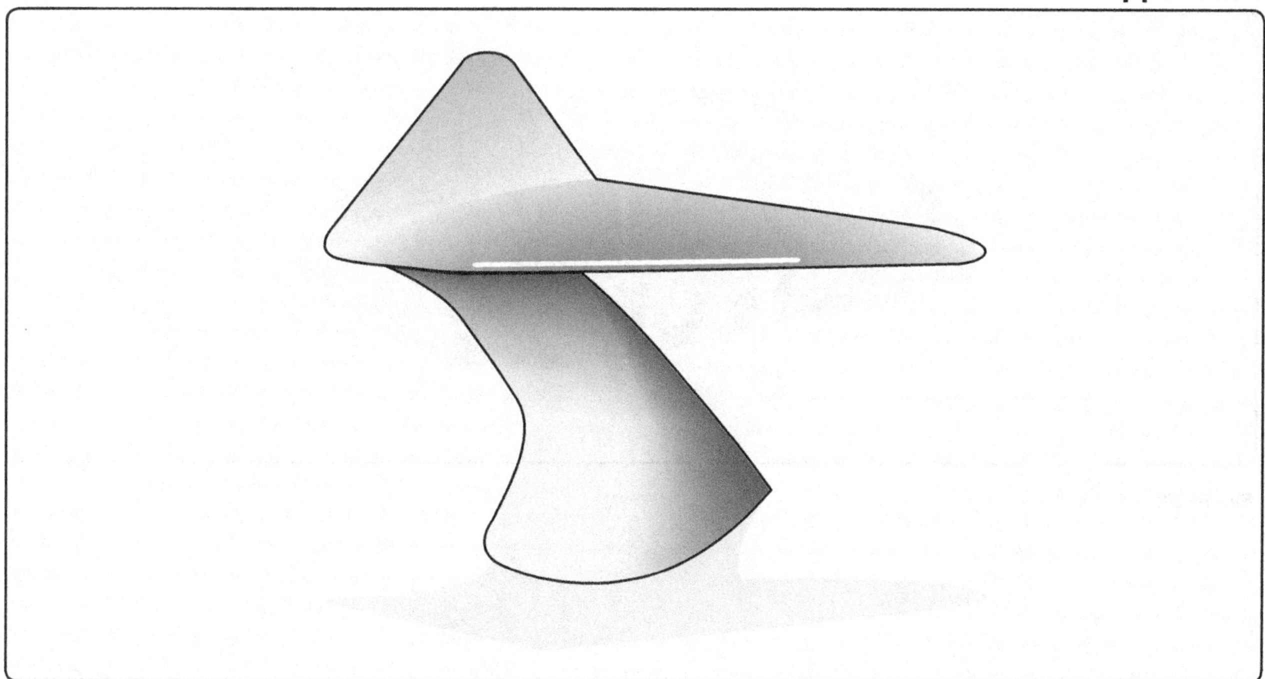

Figure 29. Antenna.

Appendix 3

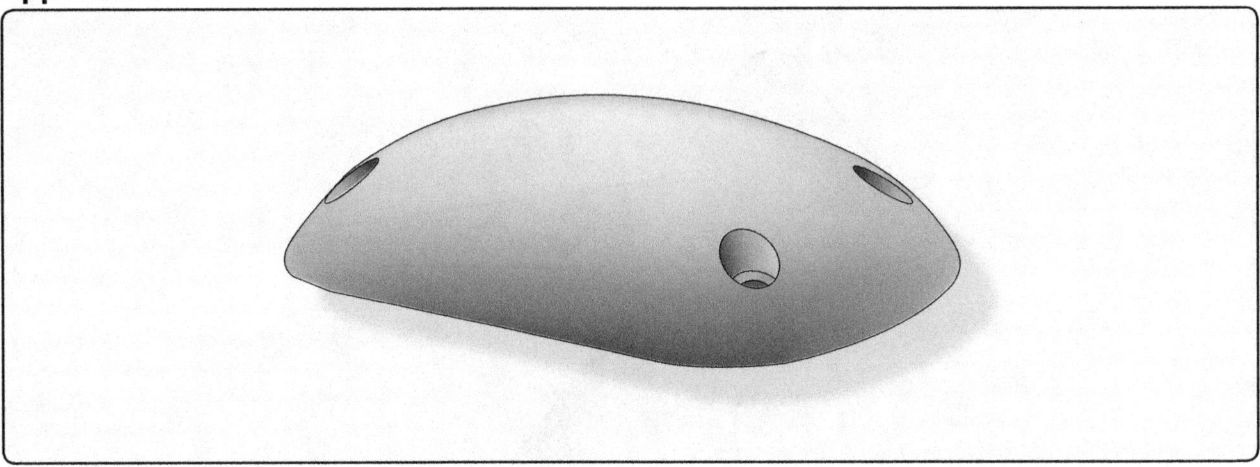

Figure 30. Antenna.

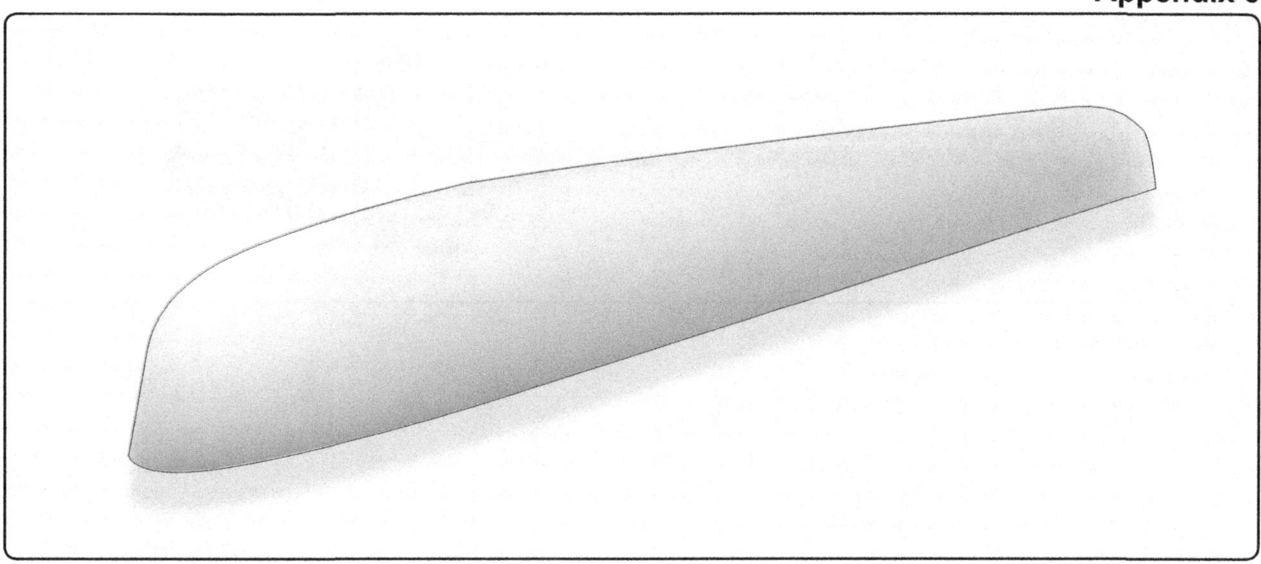

Figure 31. Antenna.

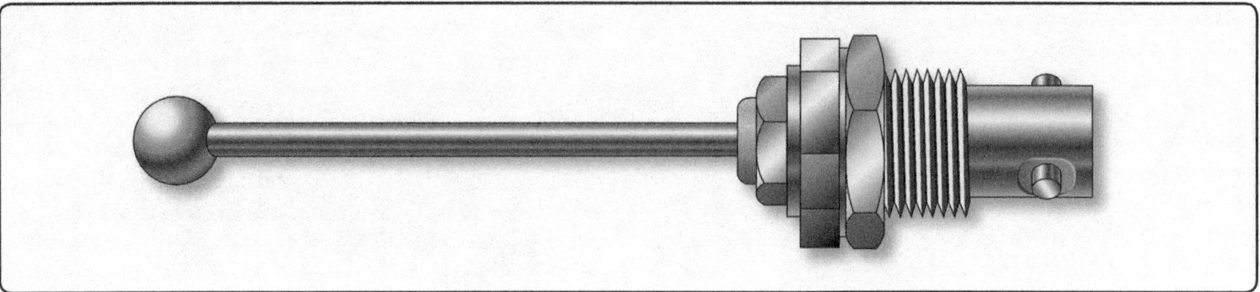

Figure 32. Antenna.

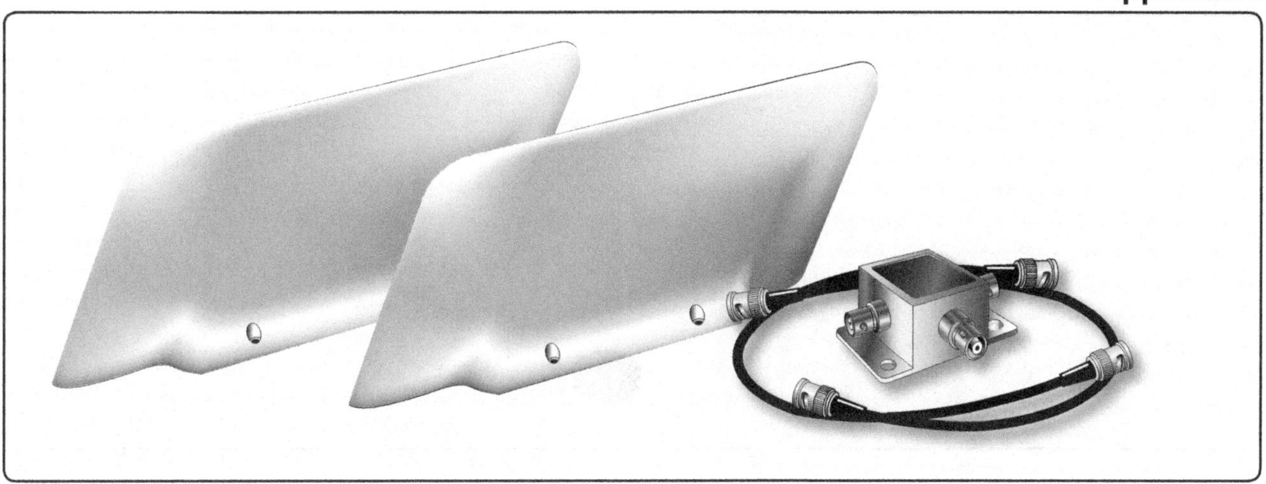

Figure 33. Antenna.

Appendix 3

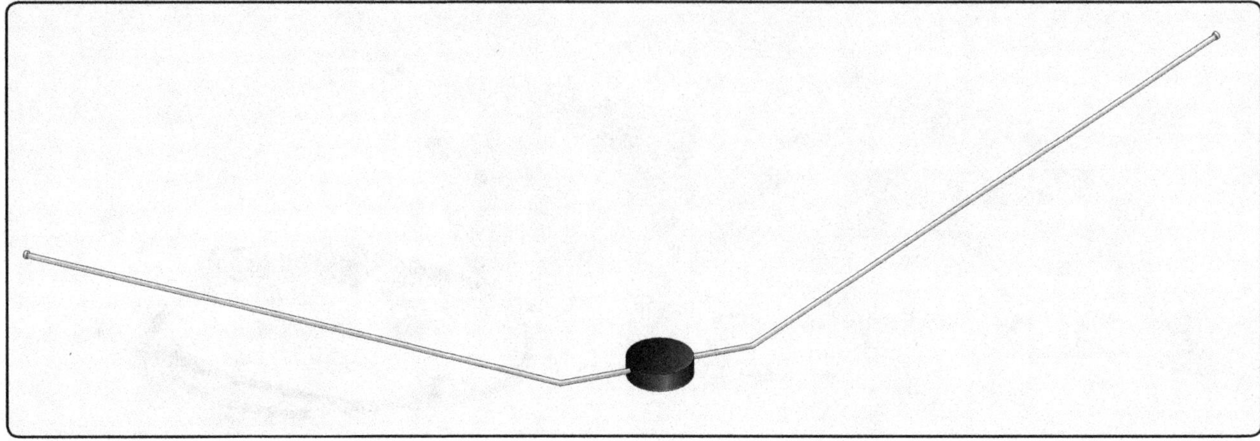

Figure 34. Antenna.

APPENDIX 4

Parachute Rigger

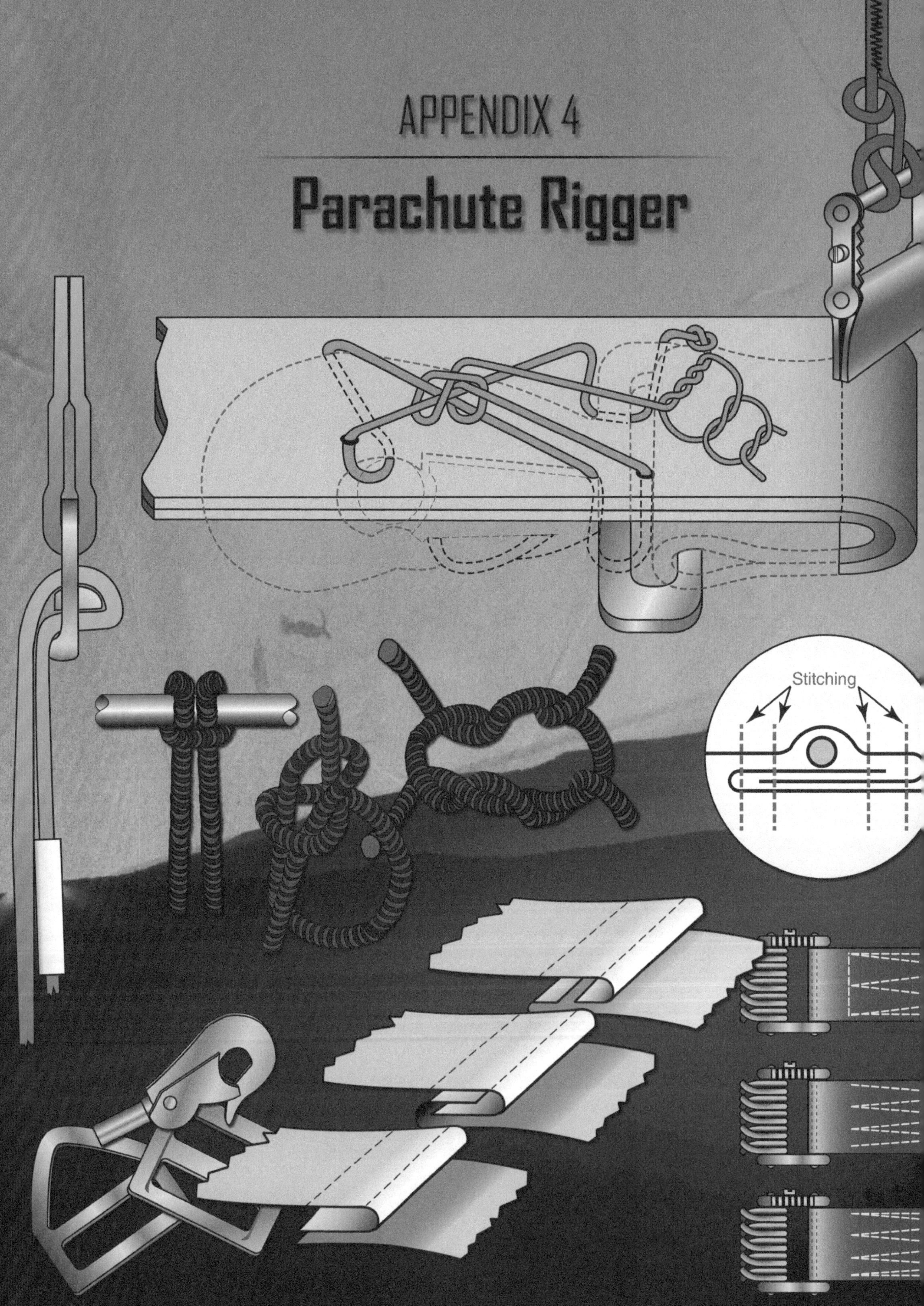

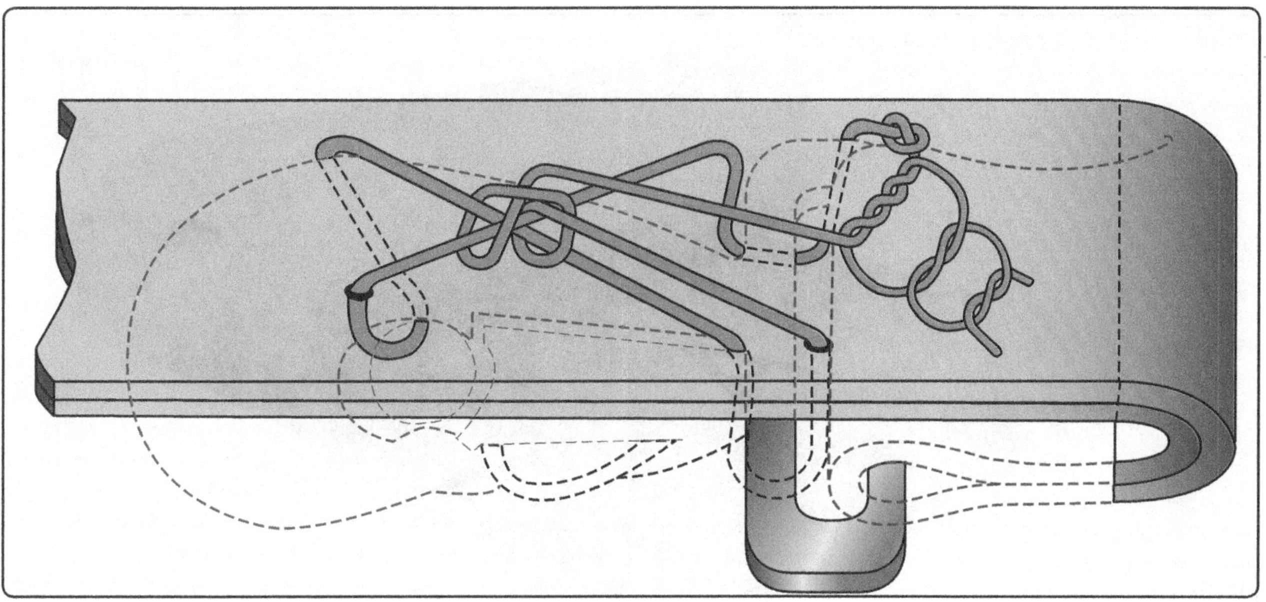

Figure 1. Tacking knot.

Appendix 4

Figure 2. Parachute material.

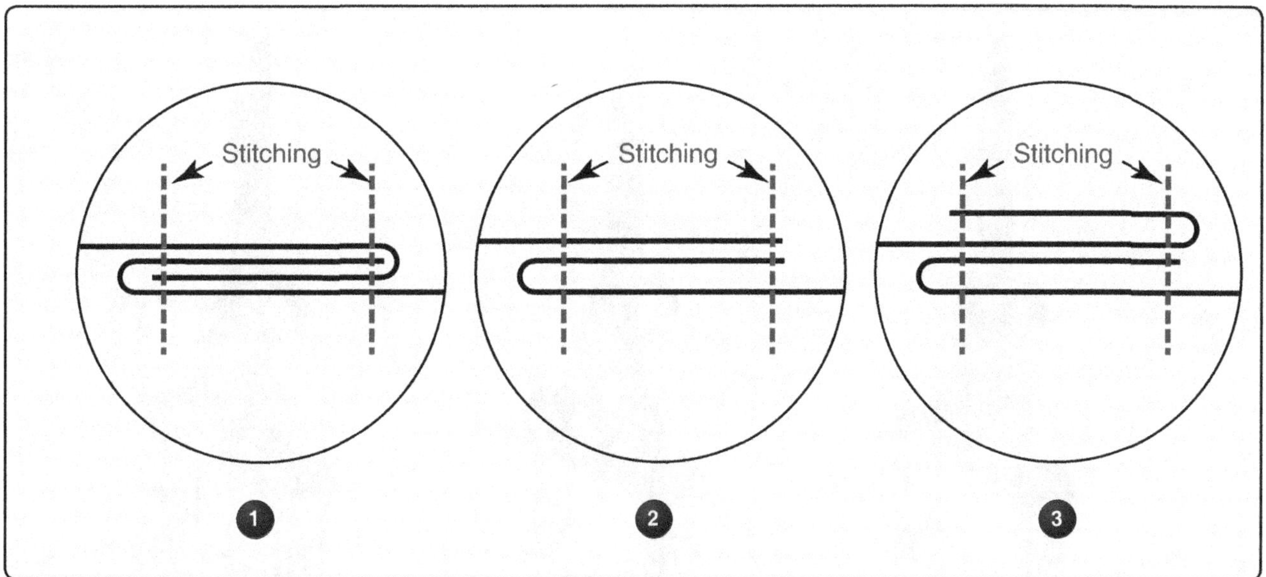

Figure 3. Seam stitching.

Appendix 4

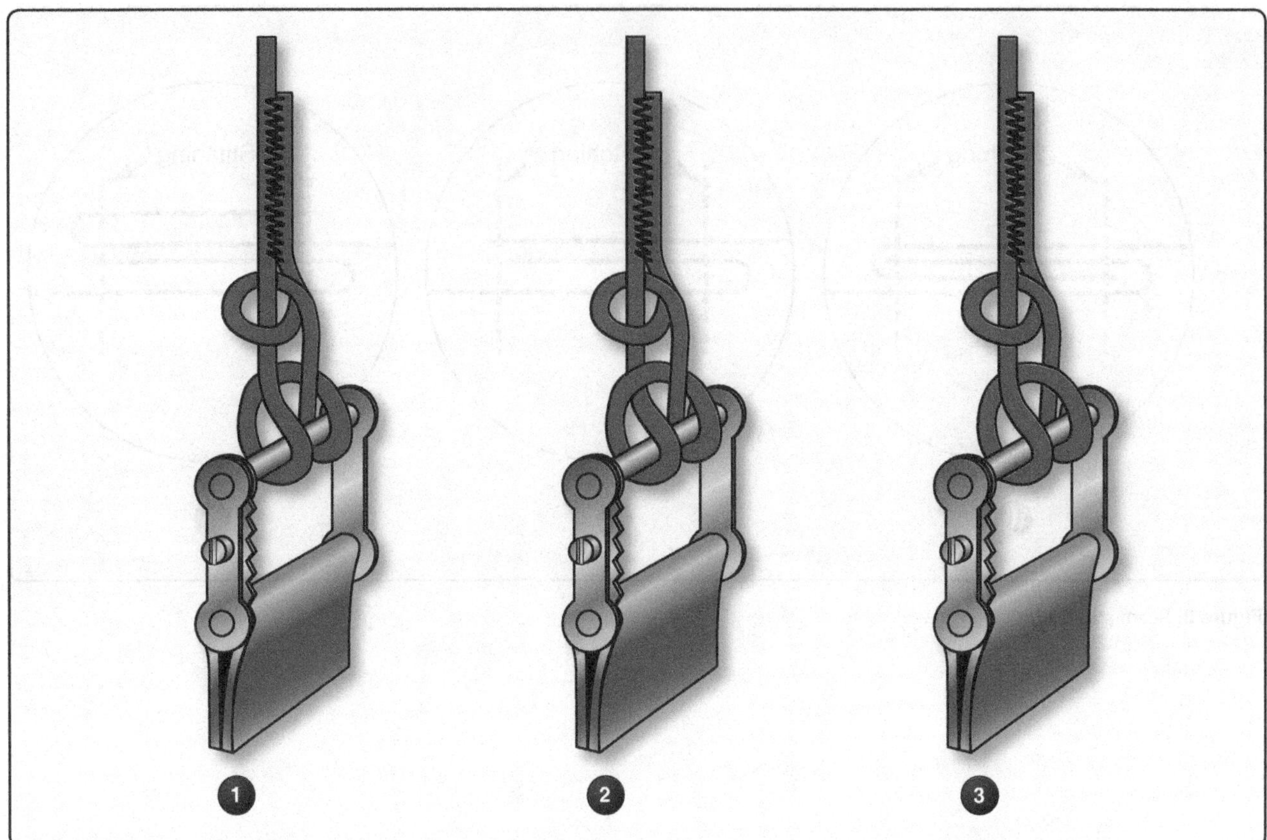

Figure 4. Suspension line attachment.

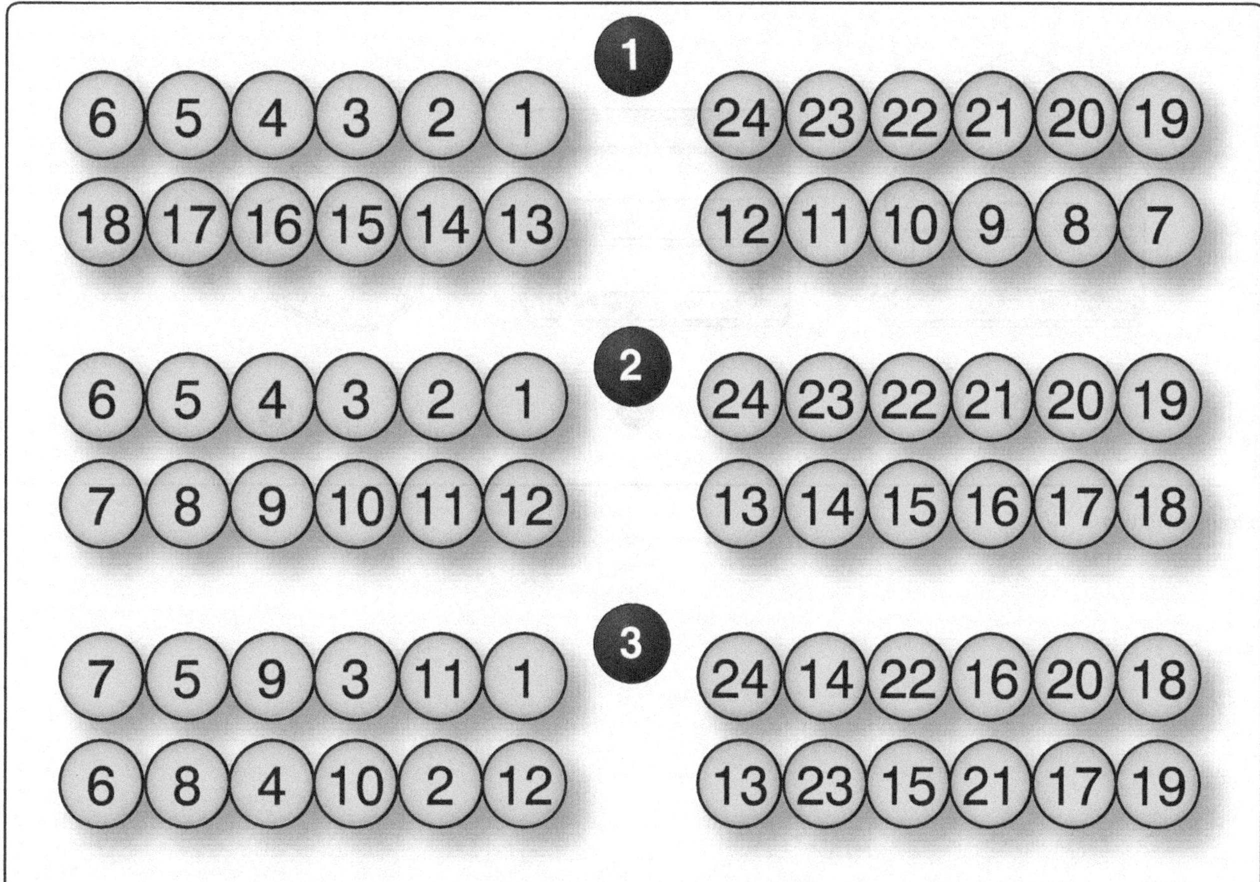

Figure 5. Suspension lines.

Appendix 4

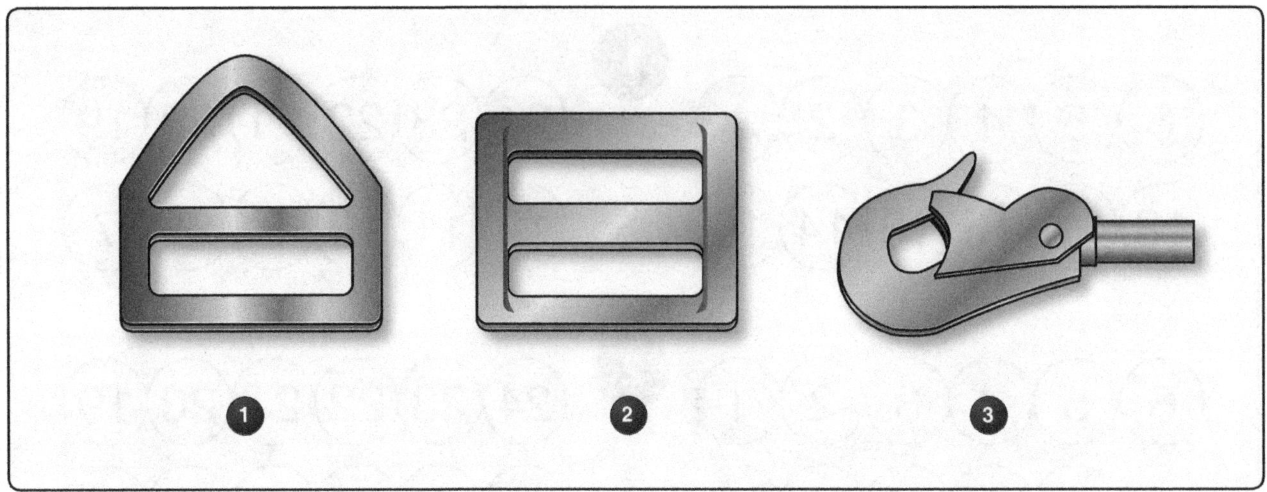

Figure 6. Fittings.

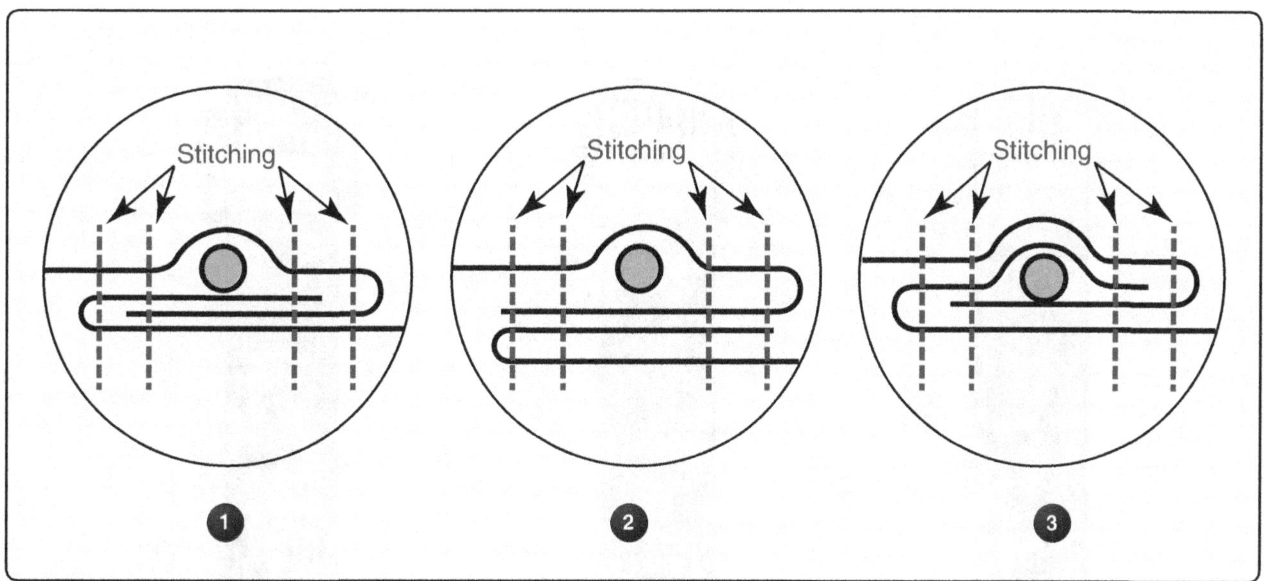

Figure 7. Radial seam stitching.

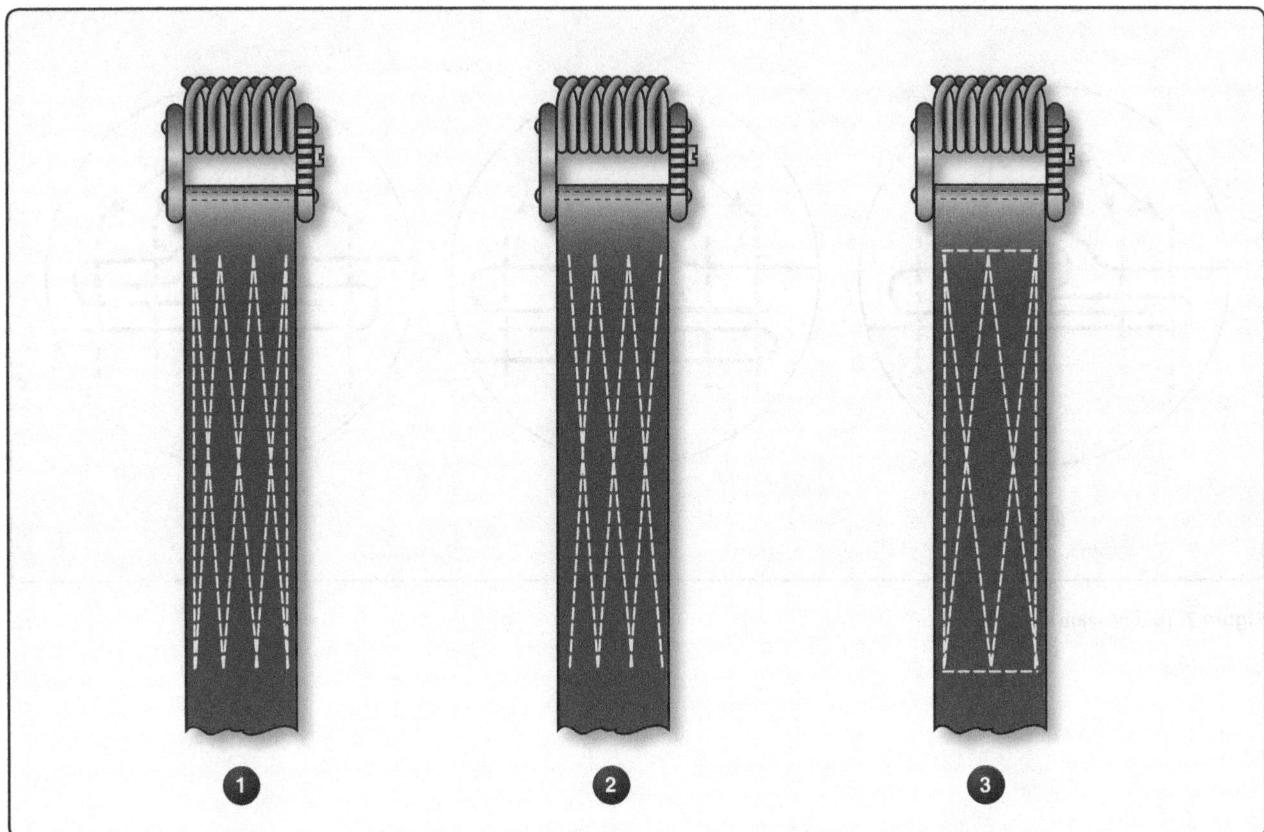

Figure 8. Lift web stitching.

Figure 9. Knots.

Appendix 4

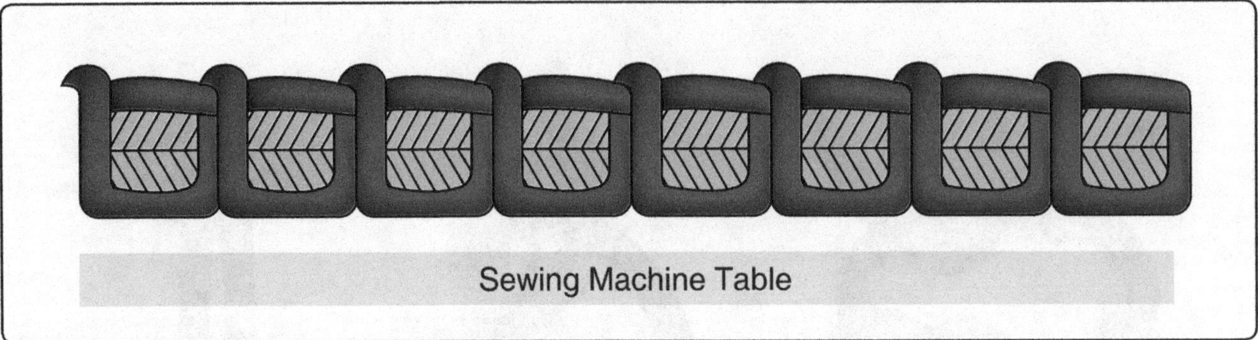

Figure 10. Machine stitching.

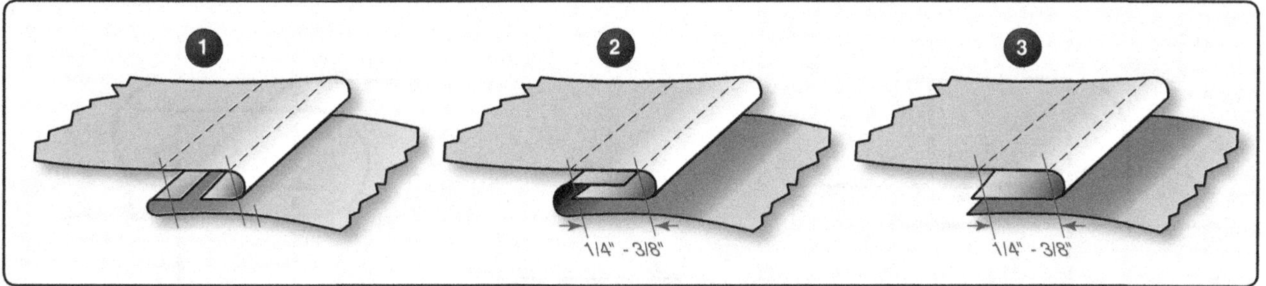

Figure 11. French fell seam.

Appendix 4

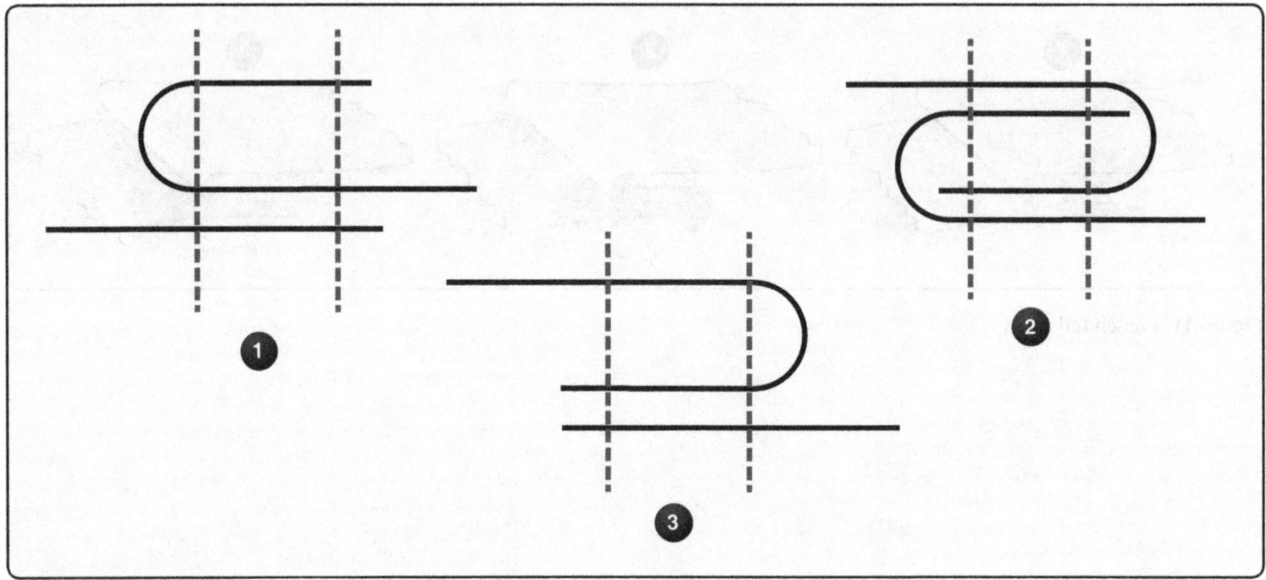

Figure 12. English fell seam.

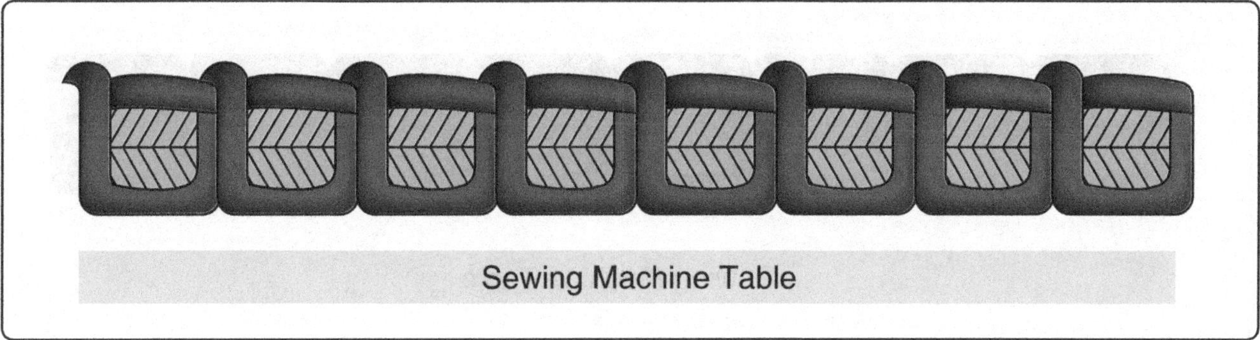

Figure 13. Machine stitching.

Appendix 4

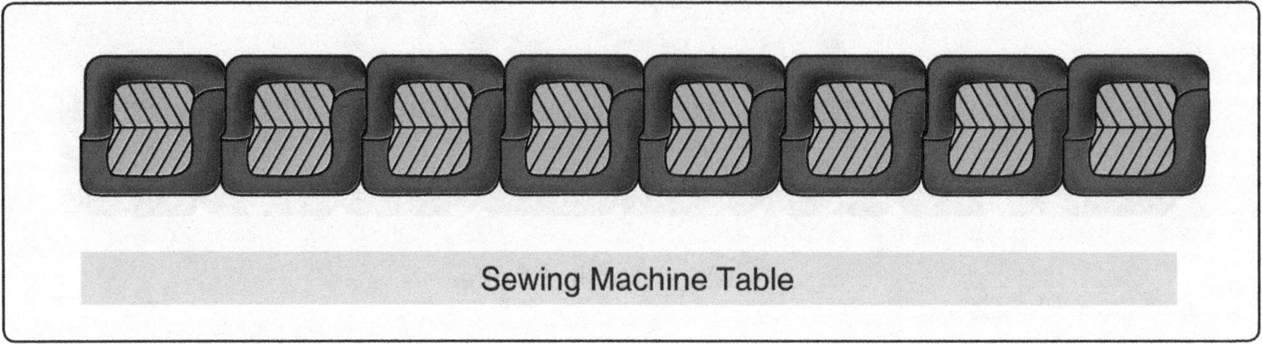

Figure 14. Machine stitching.

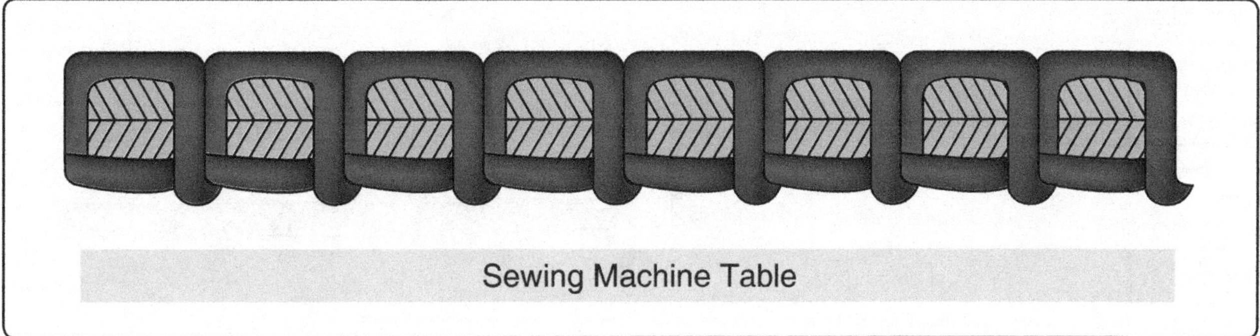

Figure 15. Machine stitching.

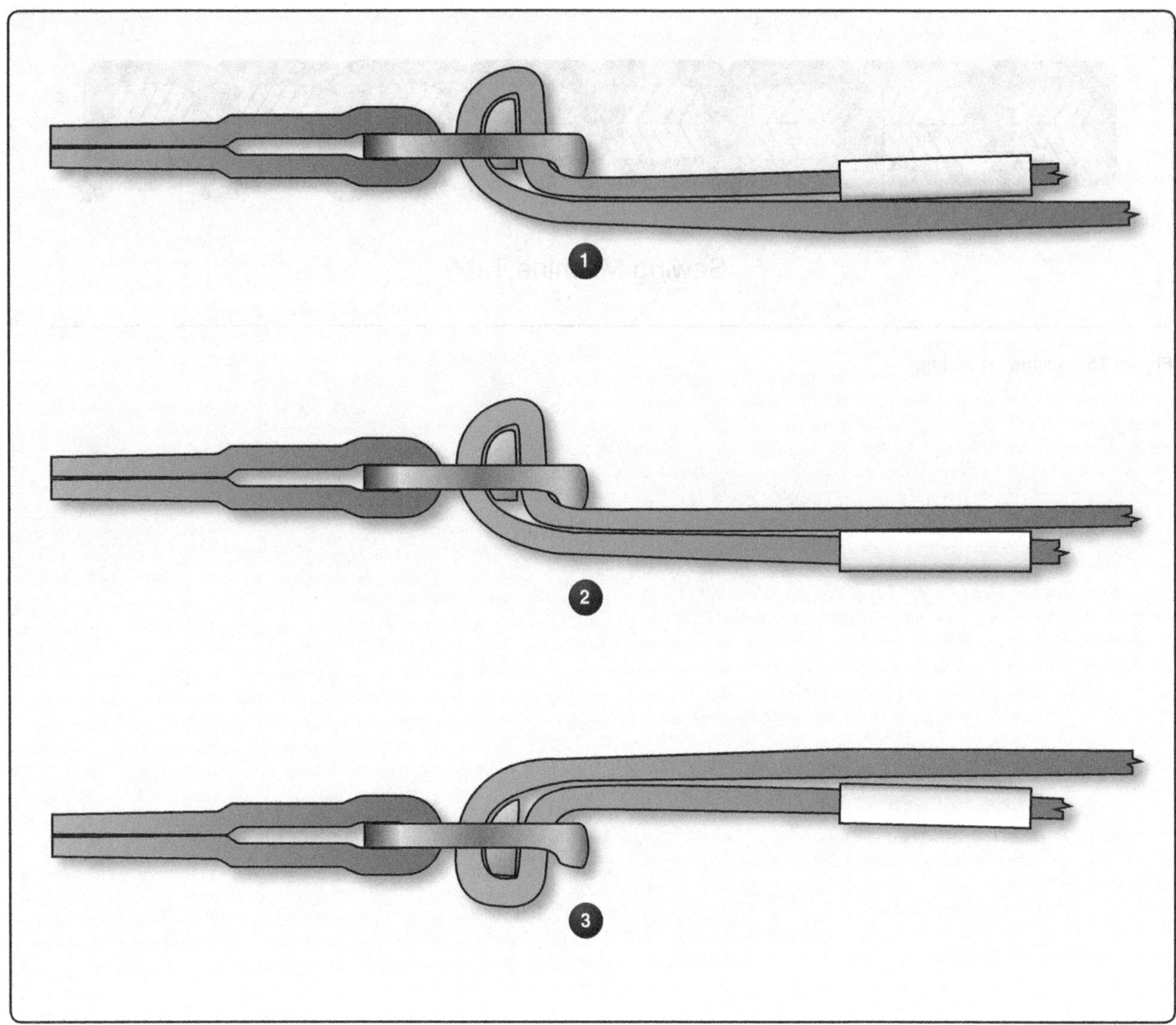

Figure 16. Hardware threading.

Made in the USA
Monee, IL
16 September 2024

65735982R00079